For People Who Love Their High-Energy, Fearful, Willful, and/or Reactive Dogs

by Eric Michael Cohen

Dog: _____

Date Started: _____

Second Edition   ©2017

www.canine-strategies.com

caninestrategies@gmail.com

Table of Contents

Preface: Tickle, Momo & Olive	2
Introduction	4
About This Workbook	5
Chapter 1: Emotion, Direction & Intensity	6
Chapter 2: [My Dog] Fell Into A Burning Ring Of Fire	11
Chapter 3: Body Language	16
Chapter 4: Preconditions	20
Chapter 5: Energy-Obedient Over Behavior-Obedient	22
Chapter 6: Our Role In The Relationship	25
Chapter 7: Confidence - Dogs That Make Good Decisions	30
Chapter 8: Become a Dog Detective (Situation-Feeling-Behavior)	34
Chapter 9: The Debate Over "Positive Reinforcement" & "Pack Leader"	38
Chapter 10: Not Carrot or Stick, Carrot and Stick	41
Chapter 11: The Power of Positivity	43
Chapter 12: Disagreements	47
Chapter 13: The Importance of Timing	51
Chapter 14: Putting it All Together	54
Chapter 15: Choose Your Battles	57
Bonus Chapter 16: Dog Geometry	59
Bonus Chapter 17: Miscellaneous Tips & Tricks	61

Preface: Tickle, Momo & Olive

"I love you mommy and daddy!"
---We love you too, Tickle.---
"I mean... I reeeaaally love you."
---We know, Tickle.---
"The first people returned me."
---That must have been horrible.---
"It was. I don't know what I did wrong. And then the second people returned me. And the third. They said I was 'unadoptable'. They said I was 'too much dog' for anyone to handle."
---They were wrong. You are perfect.---
"Really?"
---You are everything we wanted and more.---
"Really really?"
---We're never letting you go, Tickle. Ever.---
"Good. I don't think I could handle that. I love it here. I loooooove it here."
---And we love having you here. Tickle, do you want to hear a story?---
"What is it about?"
---It's about us... mommy and daddy and Tickle.---
"Yes, please. Tell me a story."
---So back before we found you, mommy and daddy were having some trouble getting along.---
"What do you mean? You love each other!"
---We do. But back then, we weren't as good at it as we are now. It was very sad. We almost weren't a family.---
"Not a family?! You mean the way people returned me? Were you going to return each other?"
---Almost, Tickle. It was a bad time.---
"Where was I during the bad time?"
---First, you were at the pound. ---
"Oh.... I remember that place. It was scary. So many other dogs. So much sadness. My friends would go away with the man and never come back..."
---Yes. You almost went with the man and never came back too. But a woman named Roslyn noticed you and called the Spotty Dog Rescue people. They came and took you out of there. Do you remember them?---
"Yes yes yes! I remember Roslyn... and Deidre and Andrea and Bob and Paul and Jim... my foster mommies and daddies!!!"
---Yes. They all fostered you. They knew you were special. They saw how much love you had to give.---
"That's right. I just want to love people. All the time. So....what was happening with you, mommy and daddy?"
---We got some help and things got better. A lot better. And when we knew we were better, we came looking for you.---
"For me? How did you know where to find me?"
---We used the computer and saw your picture and then we came to meet you. You were the gift we gave ourselves when we knew we could be a happy family again.---
"I was a gift? That's so cool! Was I a good gift?"
---The best.---
"Mommy and daddy, am I a pit bull?"
---We think so, Tickle.---
"And what is a pit bull?"
---An endless supply of love and joy on four legs.---
"That sounds like me. Is it time for kisses?"
---Always, Tickle. Always.---

It started with Tickle, one of the most exuberant dogs on the planet. My wife and I adopted her when she was roughly eighteen months. Tickle is hyper-alert, built like a professional weightlifter, and above all else, ferociously affectionate. She can launch herself, tongue-first, vertically about six feet if there is a face up there to lick. She loves people (except the mailman, men in mirrored sunglasses and anyone wearing fishing waders), loves children and likes other dogs when she is introduced properly. Whether it is her personality, her rugged good looks or a combination of both, once you meet her she is a hard dog to forget.

About a year and a half later, we added Momo to the family. After introducing Tickle to seven other potential adoptees, it was apparent when we met Momo that his personality was just right. With Tickle, Momo could be sturdy and confident enough to roll with her "bull-in-a-china-shop" energy, but he also had a more laid-back, mild-mannered side. With us, he'd be floppy, weird, gentle, and cuddly.

Two young "pit bulls" inject quite a bit of energy into the house. I'll be honest: early on, things were a bit out of hand. We needed a "canine energy management system." Sure, part of the process was about "controlling" the dogs' behavior, but the other part, maybe the more important part (we would learn), was about our energy. When we learned to set the tone of the house, sanity was restored.

Now the adventure continues with the addition of Olive, who we adopted at just eight weeks old. Olive is outgoing and incredibly friendly, with excellent dog manners. She is afraid of plastic bags and large trucks but sees the rest of the world as hers to explore. And she adores her big sister and big brother, (even if they do get annoyed with her endless energy on occasion).

I would like to thank Terrence Real, Ann Dupuis, Nancy Bersani, Rachel Golub, Betsy Vallone, Carolyn Barney, Michael Shikashio, Dana Crevling, Ken Ramirez, and especially Jim Reopelle, Deidre Croce, and Spotty Dog Rescue. Also to Sundae, Ozzy, Baxter, Sox, Denali, Montana, Finn, Carly, Bossy, Maya, Clover, Honey, Lacey, Koda, Louie, Benny, Piper, Parsli, Scampi, Ike, Chloe, and Ivy.

Above all, thank you to my wife, Bernadette, and to Tickle, Momo and Olive.

You have all contributed to this wonderful journey and I am eternally grateful.

Introduction

Most of us get a dog for the love and companionship. Dogs are really good at that stuff. And while there are times when nearly any dog can serve as a surrogate teddy bear, best friend or "fur baby," at other times they may remind us that they are still wild animals - capable of being hyperactive, terrified or aggressive - with a mouthful of razors and little to no impulse control.

It would seem simple, but integrating dogs into our lives can be extremely challenging. So, many of us consult with an "expert." And while the person we consult with may be very knowledgeable, what they tell us we "should" do is not always the same as what we are willing to do, what we are capable of doing, or what will actually be effective with our dog and our family.

I always want to understand *why* I am doing whatever I am doing. If someone is going to tell me what I *should* do, they should be ready to fit it into an explainable system so I can see the big picture. Then, let *me* decide if what is being suggested is something I am willing to do and if it is something I believe has a chance of succeeding. If a suggestion seems arbitrary, inappropriate, idiotic or if it goes against my value system, I'm not going to do it. I need to buy into the strategy if I'm going to implement it successfully.

In the search for an effective and cohesive strategy for our own dogs, my wife and I worked with a number of different dog trainers and behaviorists. Then I began a more scholarly exploration, reading everything I could get my hands on: Stanley Coren, Patricia McConnell, Pamela Dennison, Karen Pryor, Emma Parsons, Grisha Stewart, Karen Davison, Suzanne Clothier, Nicholas Dodman, Bronwen Dickey, The American College of Veterinary Behaviorists and yes, even Cesar Millan. Still not satisfied, I shadowed trainers, volunteered at a local shelter and attended dog behavior workshops and seminars, all the while looking for the elusive missing piece that would tie all this information together. And where would I find it? In my day job.

Throughout this journey, my primary vocation has been as a Marriage & Relationship Repair Specialist (www.thelifelabcoachingstudio.com) where I use an approach that combines therapy, physiology and coaching to produce long-lasting, systemic behavioral change. The more I learned about dogs, the more I saw the parallels with people. And while there are definitely parts of human psychology that show up in dog training literature, some of the sharpest tools in my relationship toolbox had yet to be incorporated when working with dogs. What I present to you in this workbook is the merging of well-established canine training and behavioral principles with an out-of-the-box approach to human relational psychology. Hopefully my perspective can expand your perspective and deliver new understanding that might aid you on your journey.

About This Workbook

The Canine Strategies Workbook is less of a "dog training book" and more of a psychological and behavioral troubleshooting guide. If you want to teach your dog to beg and roll over, you might enroll in a training class. If you want to help your dog with fear, reactivity, obsessive behaviors or hyperactivity, keep reading.

It is my intention to offer up concepts, frameworks, paradigms, and of course strategies. I'd like to give you the information you need such that you feel confident moving forward. It may be that there is only one strategy that you have been missing that will allow you to solve whatever challenge you face. Not knowing which strategy that might be, I'm not sure in which chapter you may find it. Hopefully it's in here somewhere.

There are three components to each chapter: the text, the exercises and the takeaways. The text is to educate, the exercises to personalize and the takeaways to summarize. The exercises are also available to download and print at: http://www.canine-strategies.com/exercises.html.

If a chapter doesn't seem to apply to your situation, given that they are relatively short, my recommendation would read it anyway and then to skip the exercise. There may be a nugget hiding in a seemingly unrelated chapter that gives you the breakthrough you need. Take what works for you, discard what does not, and above all, remember to enjoy your dog.

In many of the examples, I refer to the dog as "she" for consistency. Of course, everything written here applies to both genders of dogs.

There are some topics that I mention briefly about which much has been written. Clicker training and canine body language are prime examples. If you find something in these pages that interests you, look on the internet for more information. It is possible to go much deeper on many of the topics.

Some of the following concepts are quite cerebral, especially in the first chapter. There is a healthy serving of psychology contained in these pages. Hopefully, grasping these concepts will assist you in understanding what your dog might be experiencing. If something doesn't make sense, slow down and re-read it. If it still doesn't make sense, please feel free to send me an email and ask a question.

This workbook is frontloaded with information-gathering and education. Later, based on what you have come to understand about yourself and your dog, it focuses more on what you might do. Skipping to the end is not recommended. Without gathering the information that will allow you to create a solid understanding of your unique situation, you may apply the wrong tool at the wrong time and potentially make a situation worse, not better.

While the workbook is relatively short, the time to complete it will vary with each participant. Remember, your relationship with your dog is a marathon, not a sprint. Your dog's behavior is a work in progress. *Your* behavior is a work in progress. There will be steps forward and there will also be setbacks. Celebrate your victories. Learn from your missteps. The only assured way to fail is not to try.

Chapter 1: Emotion, Direction & Intensity

Your dog may hide in the laundry basket in the closet because she's scared of your three-year-old son, because she's not feeling well, or maybe just because she likes the smell of your laundry. She might bite and tug at your pant legs because she wants to play, because she wants to be fed, or because she is scared of legs. Should she be corrected, redirected or reassured? If you respond to a behavior with no understanding of why the behavior is occurring, you run the risk of creating problems instead of solving them. Punishing a scared dog doesn't make much sense, neither does rewarding an aggressive dog - and so being able to understand the instinctual and emotional motivations behind your dog's behavior would be extremely helpful when determining how to address her undesirable behaviors.

Thankfully, dogs give us some reliable indicators of how they are experiencing different situations. They "broadcast" their emotional state and relational intentions through body language and movement. We will look at body language in Chapter 3, but before we do so, let's try to understand what a dog is capable of feeling.

Emotional Range
Science shows us that in addition to a dog's instinctual (lizard) brain there is also an emotional (mammalian) brain. So to say that dogs can't feel things like we can seems unlikely. We can't know for a fact what a dog is feeling any more than we can know for a fact what another person is feeling, but based on situation, body language and behavior we can take a well-educated guess.

Emotions could be loosely defined as "the words we use to describe how we are feeling" and feelings could be described as "a construct of our physiological state." For example: you may feel happy when your serotonin level is high or anxious when your dopamine level is low. Given, the number of variations when we look at all of the hormones and neurotransmitters in the body, the number of words we use to describe our emotions is incredibly expansive: in a quick internet search, I found more than 60 words to just describe anger. When talking about dogs, it might be helpful to focus in on some of the more primary or obvious emotions. So what can dogs feel? The following graphic from an article by Stanley Coren compares the emotional development of dogs to a human child of two and a half years.

Graphic 1.1

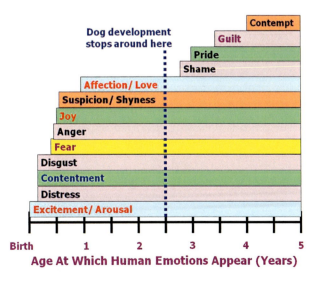

I would be tempted to also include "loss," which might also encompass sadness, loneliness and grief. (One could argue loss would fall under distress or fear of abandonment: maybe that is why it was not expressly included.)

Hormone Soup
What is the prevailing physiological state of your dog in the moment? What is happening hormonally inside your dog? Is cortisol, serotonin, dopamine or oxytocin in the driver's seat, or a combination? Let's look at a progression: from danger, to safety, to happiness, to excitement.

-"Am I in Danger?"
Just like turtles and people and bees and jellyfish, your dog is interested in staying alive: at her most instinctual level, she is on the lookout for signs of imminent danger. When she believes danger is present, her body releases stress hormones (cortisol and adrenaline) that put her into a state of high alert and often triggers her "threat response": fight, flight or freeze. What she *thinks* is a dangerous situation and what actually *is* dangerous may not be the same, so it is quite possible to have a hyper-alert dog who makes bad decisions. An example of this might be your Maltese who goes on the warpath every time your sister stops by to visit. Interestingly, it is not just about attack or invasion: threat response is also connected to abandonment and neglect, so a dog who fears abandonment may go just as far off the deep end as a dog who fears being attacked. In the modern day, for both dogs and people, this alarm system goes off far too often. For people, it goes off when we feel criticized or when our spouse forgets our birthday; for dogs, when the postman steps onto the front porch to deliver the mail or when we leave for work without them.

-"Do I Feel Safe?"
There may be no evidence of imminent danger. Still, your dog may not feel completely safe. "I don't see any strangers, other dogs or motorcycles, but one could arrive at any minute. Better keep an eye open." So while stress chemicals may be low, safety chemicals may be low as well. What is missing is reassurance, which may come in the form of a familiar location (your home or her crate), a protector (you), her favorite chew toy, etc.. When she feels reassured that she is safe, her body releases serotonin and the stress fades.

-"What Would Make Me Happy?"
So now your dog is feeling safe, but she might be bored, hungry, tired, or lonely. Some need is not met. It's not the end of the world, but things could be more enjoyable. So she does something with the intent of increasing her comfort level (and her serotonin level). Maybe she snuggles up to you on the couch. Maybe she suggests you feed her by nudging her food bowl. Maybe she paws at the door so you will let her into the yard to smell and explore. "Mom, I'm okay but I'd like to be happier. Can I have the toy/a treat/a snuggle/a walk/access to the yard/a break from the other dog? That would be really great."

-Now Amp It Up
Isn't being happy enough? Sometimes ,yes, but other times your dog wants something else: excitement, arousal, euphoria, exhilaration... Now we've got hormones all over the place (dopamine, oxytocin, norepinephrine, serotonin, adrenaline, cortisol, etc.). This could be awesome, or it could go too far and turn into a trainwreck. Either way, it's going to be intense.

Relational Direction: Towards and Away
Now, given the physiological state of your dog, what does she want to *do* in relation to the people and/or dogs around her? Would her situation improve with more interaction or less? Dogs are, in many ways, binary creatures: black or white, this or that, like or dislike. A large percentage of their behaviors

can be simplified down to a binary choice. As it relates to interactions, they will often want to:

1. Reduce distance to something desirable (such as their owner, a toy or food)
or
2. Increase distance from something undesirable (motorcycles, tall men, other dogs, etc.)

Let's take the example of your dog walking on leash as you approach another on-leash dog. In nature, if your dog was scared or unsure about the other dog, she could simply move away, but given the constraints of the leash, that option is unavailable. So she might try the opposite: barking and lunging *in hopes the other dog will back away*. Then something unexpected happens: *you* pull her away from the other dog. Now your dog has learned that barking and lunging at the unsafe thing will result in an increase in distance, thanks to you. Each time she sees a scary dog, she repeats the behavior, and each time she repeats the behavior, you pull her away. The thought process locks in: bark and lunge to increase distance.

Imagine a similar situation, but with one major difference: your dog is not scared but instead playful or curious and wants to get close to the other dog. When she sees the other dog, she starts pulling and barking. This time, when you pull her away, it is a punishment instead of a reward: "Mommy, I want to get close to that dog! I want to play with that dog!!!!!" Same behavior, completely different intent. When we add body language to our skill set (Chapter 3), the intent will become much clearer.

(Direction (towards or away) + Emotion (fear or joy)) x Intensity=?
There's quite a bit going on here. You might be thinking, "Do I need a degree in algebra to understand my dog?" No, of course not - but a way to explain it all would be helpful. Let's take what we have discussed already in this chapter, simplify it, and hopefully make it easy to remember. (For visual learners, there are some graphics coming up that should be quite helpful.)

This is how we will plot Direction:
1. **Up:** Joy, happiness, contentment, safety, etc.
2. **Down:** Fear, concern, anxiety, suspicion, etc.
3. **Left:** Avoidance, desire to increase distance from something, desire to be alone, etc.
4. **Right:** Invasion, desire to reduce distance to something, desire to be close to, etc.

And this is how we will plot Intensity:
1. **Balance:** Basic needs are met, excitement level is at or near zero. Neither fearful nor joyful.
2. **Engaged:** Something of interest is going on: receiving affection, hearing a sound outside, seeing another dog, being told to sit, chewing on a toy, etc. Mild to moderate intensity.
3. **Over Threshold:** Panic, terror, rage, aggression, obsession, hyperactivity, etc.. In this state it is difficult if not impossible to communicate with the dog.

The Goal: A Balanced & Engaged Dog
For most of us, I would expect our goal would be having a dog that moves between Balance and Engaged most of the time (and maybe occasionally riding the edge of hyperactive or hyper-affectionate, assuming everyone stays safe). It is normal for dogs (and people) to feel a wide range of emotions, and so long as the intensity in any given direction doesn't go too far, everything should be fine. Focusing first on Balance (the white circle in the center) and Engaged (in gray), let's start by looking at a range of mild to moderate emotional states in Graphic 1.2:

Graphic 1.2

☐ Balance (baseline)

▨ Engaged (healthy range of feelings/behaviors)

We can use so many different anthropomorphic* words to characterize our dog's behaviors and personality. The words in the gray Engaged range are descriptive while also being somewhat subjective. As we move farther from Balance in the center, we get closer and closer to Over Threshold, which will be the focus in Chapter 2.

*Anthropomorphic: having qualities usually attributed to humans

Exercise 1: Emotion, Direction & Intensity

First of all, congratulations for making it through Chapter 1! Let's get started with the first exercise. (If you would like to print out the exercises, a downloadable PDF can be found at http://www.canine-strategies.com/exercises.html.)

1. List three or four pleasurable anthropomorphic* adjectives you would use to describe your dog (Ex: Goofy, spirited, loving, sweet)

   _____

2. List three or four undesirable anthropomorphic* adjectives you would use to describe your dog (Ex: Bossy, disobedient, crazy, petrified)

   _____

   Anthropomorphic: having qualities usually attributed to humans

3. Create a sentence that will be your goal for this workbook. For example, "I would like my bossy, dominant and sometimes aggressive dog to be more calm," or "I would like my terrified, anxious, unsettled dog to be more confident and playful." You might combine your answers from questions 1 and 2, or start from scratch.

   _____

   _____

   _____

Takeaway
Thinking of a dog's emotional development in terms similar to that of a human child gives us a framework for discussion. We may also gain insight from understanding that connected to our dog's physiological/emotional state (fear, joy, and all other emotions) there is a directional component of reducing or increasing distance to dogs, people, and other elements of her environment.

Chapter 2: ☐ [My Dog] Fell Into A Burning Ring Of Fire ☐
(a Johnny Cash reference)

Graphic 2.1

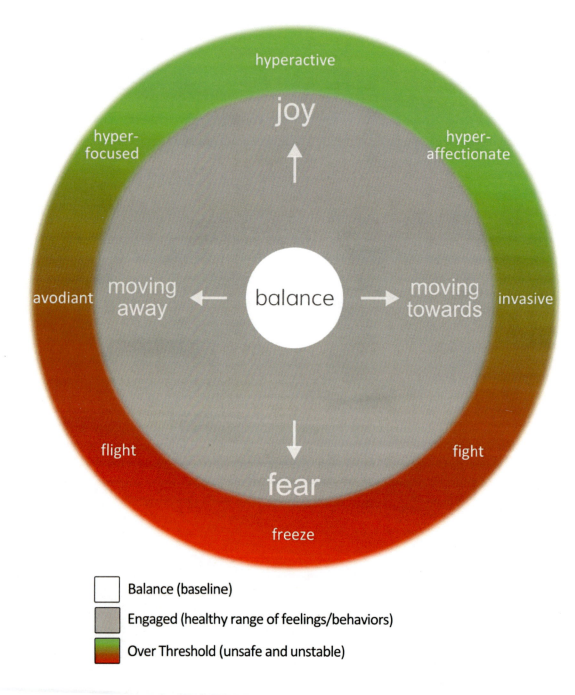

Over Threshold, the outer ring on Graphic 2.1 describes a range of different extreme energy states. While there may be times when entering these states does not cause a problem, a chronic predisposition in any of these directions may be why you picked up this workbook. At the bottom of the ring we have the "threat responses": fight, flight and freeze. Let's go around the ring, starting at the top, moving clockwise.

↑ Hyperactive (Joy)

"I'm a crazy lab running around the dog park! Are we chasing or playing or fighting? I don't know! I've forgotten all the rules of socialization!! Baaahhhhhh!!!" Your dog may not be scared or angry but may incite fear or anger in other dogs. And, another dog's fear or anger may shift your dog's direction from hyperactive to a threat response (fight, flight, freeze). Mania in a vacuum may not be a big deal, such as the dog running around your backyard by herself, but if someone were to unexpectedly open the gate, the dog could bolt out of the yard at full speed into traffic.

Related behaviors: "the zoomies," inability to sit still, play that is too intense for the other dog, etc.

↗ Hyper-Affectionate (Joy + Moving Towards)

Sounds great, right? Not if the source of the affection is a person who is afraid of dogs, or if the affection is too strong or intense for the recipient. You may like when your dog licks your face and when she is excited to greet you when you come home, but if her exuberance is too much, she might hit you in the face with her snout or inadvertently scratch you with a paw. This is especially dangerous with large dogs and small children: the dog may have no intention to inflict harm, but harm may be the result.

Related behaviors: intense greeting rituals, excessive face-licking, need to always be with you, etc..

→ Invasive (Moving Towards)

Between affection and aggression, this is the energy of a dog who lacks boundaries or consideration for personal space. This dog may approach other dogs, completely oblivious to whether or not the other dog is interested in interacting. Another example would be a dog that claims space (on the couch, in the front seat of the car) just because she wants to be there, not because she want to be affectionate or cuddly.

Related behaviors: a dog who is "always moving forward," stealing (food from the counter, toys from another dog), intrusive behavior, etc.

↘ Fight (Fear + Moving Forwards)

Aggression is almost always undesirable from our dogs. It might be a dog that is overprotective of her owner or a dog that aggressively barks and pulls on the leash; a dog that charges strangers at the door or a dog that pins other dogs at the dog park. Above all, a dog that is willing to bite is a danger to its family, other dogs and to itself. Fight is a *willingness* to move forwards but often with the *desire* that the target back down or move away. If the other dog shows its own intensity moving forward, there may be a fight. "Don't even think about it!" might be what a person would say in a similar situation as an attempt to diffuse through a show of strength.

Related behaviors: aggressive barking, pulling, charging, snapping, fighting, biting, etc.

↓ Freeze (Fear)

A dog that suddenly goes stiff; eyes fixed, tail straight and motionless, mouth closed; may appear calm to the untrained eye, but to someone who can read body language this is the sign of a dog that does not know what to do. This dog is unpredictable. It could retreat, it could attack, it could relax, or it could start running at full speed. Freeze is fear combined with confusion or indecision, elevated to a tipping point. Another way to think of freeze is as emotional and physical paralysis. When your dog is confronted with something she finds threatening, she may feel paralyzed: "Do I fight or flee? I don't know! I'm just going to shut down!" This strategy might work - the scary thing might go away - or, by neither escalating nor diffusing, staying there might prolong the conflict. And if freeze doesn't work, your dog might be forced to fight. Dogs often momentarily freeze when playing, dancing between flee and fight, but the emotional intensity is low and the dog does not feel unsafe to the point of needing to

protect itself.
Related behaviors: paralysis, lying down or going completely rigid in a stressful situation, urination, etc.

↙ Flight (Fear + Moving Away)
"Get me out of here!" The safest thing to do when confronted with perceived danger might be to leave. Creating distance is fine, but an Over Threshold dog who is running from danger may actually induce a desire to chase, or she might be so fixated on getting away that she ignores her surroundings (gets lost, gets hit by a car, etc.). Also included in flee is hiding. You may be experiencing flight in your dog who is scared of things that are not actually dangerous but that she perceives as dangerous. This is also often the realm of phobias.
Related behaviors: hiding, retreating, cowering, fearful barking ("If I can't leave, could you please leave?"), etc.

← Avoidant (Moving Away)
Avoidant behavior is a degree less fearful than flight but equally if not more distant. Your dog might be thinking, "I'm not really scared by that person/dog, but I have no interest in interacting with him." Certain breeds are more predisposed to being on the avoidant side of the scale, such as Akitas and Chow Chows, but if it gets to the point that your dog doesn't ever want to be around you, or if she is completely tuned out and disinterested in you, this can be a problem. It might be helpful to look at why the dog is so avoidant. Does she see you/another dog as too intrusive or controlling? If so, she goes the other way.
Related behaviors: lack of interest in you/other dogs, lack of obedience (never comes when called), etc.

↖ Hyper-Focused (Joy + Moving Away)
Obsessions, compulsions, and fixations: your dog is deriving so much enjoyment from the behavior at hand such that you have disappeared from her universe. It is okay for your dog to be happy doing something by herself, so long as it is not Over Threshold. It is not that the behavior is inherently dangerous, but the level of intensity makes it dangerous. Hyper-Focused is also the realm of prey drive: everything else fades into the background when your dog gets fixated on a bird or squirrel.
Related behaviors: obsessive grooming, tail-chasing, digging, chasing/stalking prey, toy obsession, etc.

Danger on "The Ring Of Fire": Shifting Direction While Over Threshold
Direction can shift quickly while maintaining intensity level. For example: two hyperactive dogs are playing, running at top speed and alternately chasing each other, when a new dog suddenly appears and surprises one of the dogs. The surprised dog, already hyper-excited, now feels fear and flips to aggression or terror (fight or flight) without warning. In a less excited state, the dog may not have had any reaction to the appearance of a new playmate, but when Over Threshold, things can change at lightning speed.

"Don't worry. My dog is friendly!" is often heard right before a hyperactive dog gets in another dog's personal space. If I ran across a field at top speed and came to within inches of your face, I doubt that a smile on my face would keep you from feeling or reacting defensively. Intensity levels can be contagious: between dogs, between people and between dogs and people.

People are also capable of shifting direction when over threshold. When a sports team wins the game that captures the title such as the World Series, Super Bowl or Stanley Cup, the celebration by the winning team's fans can turn violent, such as flipping over cars and lighting them on fire. Their joy and the contagious quality of that level of over-excitement (and probably quite a bit of alcohol) creates the perfect storm for a gross lack of judgement.

Common Terms
There are a few terms that are commonly used in dog training literature that overlap with some of the concepts in the first two chapters. In case these words had been floating around in your head while reading, I'll address them here and then we can move on.

-"Fear Aggression"
An overused term in the world of dog training is "fear aggression." Determining if the dog is angry or fearful may be difficult; my strong assumption is that both fear and anger are present in most violent incidents. I find the term "threat response" to be much less confusing. Expressions of fear and aggression are common between dogs in varying degrees. They are not inherently "bad." A growl that requests another dog back off is a healthy expression to avoid violence. Some dogs display anger (barking, leaning forward. etc.) without ever getting violent, just as some other dogs don't overtly show aggression before launching an attack. Offensive behavior can be used for defense and defensive behavior can be used to mask imminent offense. An Over Threshold threat response can be violent - it can also trigger violence from another dog - so keeping our dogs under threshold is an important part of keeping them safe.

-"Dominance" & "Submission"
These terms are also quite common in dog literature. I have heard people say, "You have a dominant dog." I disagree. What is more accurate is that I have a dog that in the moment may be acting in a more dominant or invasive manner. For example, when Tickle is with most other dogs, she is usually confident and a bit bossy, but when she is around Finn (a much smaller dog she lived with in a foster situation) she shows immediate submission. Similarly, for those who like to think in terms of pack structure, Tickle may sometimes appear more like the leader and at other times more like the follower depending on who else is around (dogs or people). Also, there are times when Momo or Olive will correct Tickle's behavior and then return to their more common submissive roles. The long and the short of it: the pack order or hierarchy between dogs and people may shift as new members enter the equation or when the energy of an existing member shifts. "Dominance" and "submission" exist on a sliding scale, not as absolutes.

Exercise 2: The Ring Of Fire

1. Which directions on "The Ring Of Fire" are you most concerned about with your dog? Circle all that apply. If there is one direction that is by far the most troublesome, draw a star next to it.
    a. ↑ Hyperactive (Joy)
    b. ↗ Hyper-Affectionate (Joy + Moving Towards)
    c. → Invasive (Moving Towards)
    d. ↘ Fight (Fear + Moving Forwards)
    e. ↓ Freeze (Fear)
    f. ↙ Flight (Fear + Moving Away)
    g. ← Avoidant (Moving Away)
    h. ↖ Hyper-Focused (Joy + Moving Away)

2. Have you ever seen your dog shift direction when Over Threshold? If so, from what to what? For example: from Fight to Flight, From Flight to Avoidance, etc.

    _____
    _____

3. Are there certain situations where your dog is very likely to go Over Threshold? For example: meeting strange dogs, thunder, seeing the mailman through the window, when the vacuum cleaner is on, when her favorite people come to visit, when she finds a new stick, etc.

    _____
    _____

Takeaway

Doing whatever we can to keep our dog from going Over Threshold (keeping her out of The Ring Of Fire) gives us the best chance of having a safe and happy dog. Fight and Flight aren't the only states to be concerned with; there are many different versions of Over Threshold.

Chapter 3: Body Language

Dogs aren't very capable of communicating how they feel through verbal language, but they are constantly communicating through body language. If one wanted to understand someone who only spoke sign language, it would be helpful to learn sign language. Similarly, learning to recognize your dog's physical communications will assist in understanding what your dog is thinking and feeling.

Body Language: Take Your Dog's T-E-M-P
A wagging tail indicates some form of excitement, but not always joy. A panting dog with its tongue hanging out may be happy, excited, stressed, content, tired or overheated. Each of the items below tells part of the story but it is the *combination* of body parts; Tail, Eyes & Ears, Mouth, and Posture, (T-E-M-P); that forms the complete picture. Thinking back to the first two chapters, note that some of the items below are good indicators of intensity, while others correlate better to direction.

Tail
- Up: excited/aroused/alert/suspicious
- Horizontal: engaged/attentive/interested
- Down but not tucked: balanced/calm/content/happy
- Tucked: stress/anxiety/fear/submission
- Still & Relaxed: balanced/calm/content
- Still & Stiff: suspicious/defensive/unsure/anxious/alert
- Loose Wag: happy/playful/excited
- Stiff Wag (deliberately flits back and forth): precursor to threat response/ angry/trapped/afraid/frustrated

Eyes
- Looking Directly Towards: desiring engagement (affection/interaction/conflict)
- Looking Away: desiring space (conflict-avoidant/fear/shutdown/submission)
- Soft Gaze: balanced/relaxed/content/happy
- Hard Stare: suspicious/alert/fixated/tense/aggressive
- Dilated: aroused/fearful/stressed/threatened
- Partially Closed: submissive/deferential/fearful/anxious
- Whale Eyed: threat response/terrified/frozen/cornered/not wanting to but ready to attack

Ears
- Up & Forward: alert/interested/suspicious/aggressive
- Up & Relaxed: calm/happy/balanced
- Back: friendly/submissive/affectionate
- Back & Flattened: threat response/terrified/paralyzed/defensive but ready to fight

Mouth
- Closed: relaxed/aware/interested/cautious/anxious/alert/suspicious
- Slightly Open: tongue partially visible: relaxed/calm/content/curious
- Open (with tongue clearly visible): happy/excited/stressed/hot
- Narrowly Open with lips curled back to expose teeth: unsure/fearful/concerned/trapped/ "Please back off!"
- Wide Open (C-shaped) with lips pulled back to expose lots of teeth: angry and ready to fight

Posture
- Leaning Forward: interested/confident/alert/suspicious/defensive/aggressive/excited
- Balanced Posture (equal weight front to back): calm/content/happy/safe/alert/cautious
- Leaning Back: playful submission
- Rolling Over to Expose Belly: playful submission/appeasement/de-escalation
- Intent to Appear Bigger (head up, ears up, strong posture): bossy/dominant/aggressive
- Intent to Appear Smaller (head down, ears down, tail down, possibly one paw raised): deferential/timid/submissive/afraid

I know… there is quite a bit to remember and some of it might seem contradictory. Start by observing element by element. Watch your dog's tail one day, then watch her ears the next day. Watch her mouth the next day and her eyes the day after that. Just like learning a verbal language, it takes practice. It will become easier to process multiple elements once you have a grasp on each.

Thankfully, much of canine body language becomes quite a bit more intuitive when you compare it to human behavior. If I wanted you to back off and I thought a show of force was my best chance, I'd stare you straight in the eyes, stand tall, hold my head up, and try to project as much confidence as possible. If I was a dog, I would do all that and in addition thrust my ears forward and wag my tail very deliberately. In contrast, if I wanted to play, I would do everything I could to express my joy and excitement with a non-threatening gaze, a loose posture, a relaxed wagging tail, and a tongue hanging out. If that didn't work I might taunt you a little, but not too much… I want to play, not fight.

Graphic 3.1 on the next page shows Tickle in a variety of poses. Depending on your dog and her breed, some signs may be easy to read, others more difficult. For example, the body language of a dog with a curly tail or floppy ears may take more time to learn. Also, be aware that dogs' energy (direction & intensity) can change quite rapidly. You may witness a few different poses in a matter of seconds. This is especially true during play. In fact, a great way to observe body language is to go to a dog park without your dog to watch other dogs interact.

Most people know to stay away from a dog who is barking and on high alert. Fewer people recognize the signs of a dog that is very uncomfortable and would like to escape the situation or be left alone. Recognizing when a dog needs space and when a dog is feeling anxious or stressed may give us the opportunity to intervene before the situation escalates. Pay particular attention to "Please Leave Me Alone" (in the middle row). "The dog just bit without warning!" is often not the case; more accurately, the dog bit after giving signs *the only way it knew how,* which the human was unable to read.

Also note that the dog exposing her belly (top row) in "Submissive/Happy/I'm Not A Threat" may be feeling playful, wanting affection, showing submission or trying to avoid conflict. Just like human emotions, context is very important.

One last thing to consider: an element might tell you more about what the dog *isn't* saying. Take a closed mouth, for example. It could mean relaxed, aware, interested, cautious, anxious, alert or suspicious. That's a pretty wide range, but none of those things are extreme. A closed mouth may be a poor indicator of direction, but a great indicator of intensity: "My dog may be anxious, alert, or suspicious, but her mouth is closed so I don't think she's to the point of terrified, hyperactive, or violent."

This graphic just scratches the surface of canine body language. If you would like to learn more, I highly recommend a Google Images search for "dog body language" or reading the book "How to Speak Dog" by Stanley Coren.

Graphic 3.1:

Exercise 3: Body Language

1. What part(s) of your dog do you find easiest to read? Tail? Eyes? Ears? Mouth? Posture? Learning to read *your dog's* body language is incredibly important. Spend a day observing each element. Monday, watch her tail; Tuesday, her ears; etc. Situationally or environmentally, what is happening when her tail goes up or down? What is happening when her ears go up or back? This exercise can actually be quite a bit of fun, especially if you can involve the rest of the family or a friend. Watching the parts is like learning words; watching the whole dog merges the words into understandable phrases.

2. Over the course of the next few weeks, observe your dog's body language. Check off each posture on the chart below as you learn to recognize it. Circle the postures that precede any unwanted behavior. Note the situation(s) in which the behavior was observed. Recognizing these moments will come into play in later chapters.

Pose	Situation(s) observed
Relaxed (down)	
Relaxed	
Submissive or Happy or I'm Not A Threat	
Happy	
Ready To Play	
Submissive or Deferential	
Please Leave Me Alone	
Anxious or Stressed	
Terrified	
Fearful Ready To Fight	
Alert	
Wary or Unsure or Suspicious	
Stalking	
Defensive or Territorial	
Angry Ready To Fight	

Takeaway
Our dogs are constantly expressing their emotional state through body language. We simply need to become more adept at recognizing it.

Chapter 4: Preconditions

Up to this point, we've looked at understanding our dog's physiological, emotional and relational and state. Before we dig into what to do, let's make sure your dog is not acting up for any of the following physical reasons. Sometimes what we perceive to be behavioral problems are actually health problems or environmental deficiencies. *This chapter is especially important if you have seen a sudden and extreme shift in your dog's behavior.*

A Very Important Note About Exercise
The daily lives of humans are filled with all sorts of experiences: challenges, stresses, victories, setbacks, surprises, travel, etc. Meanwhile, your dog may have spent the entire day in her crate or home alone, doing nothing. You get home and want to relax. She sees your return as the beginning of her day. If you are not exercising your dog (and I don't mean taking her out just long enough to do her business), stop reading this book and walk or run with her every day for a week. You may not have to do much more work than that to fulfill her basic needs and stop her from acting like a tornado every night. *A tired dog is almost always a happy dog.*

Exercise 4: Preconditions Checklist

1. Check any items that need further consideration:

Health: Are there any health issues that might be affecting your dog's mood? A dog in pain may become aggressive, fearful or avoidant. If so, schedule a vet appointment and see what might be affecting her behavior.

- ❏ Skin (rash, allergy, ear infection, etc.)
- ❏ Teeth (cavity, decay, abscess, etc.)
- ❏ Muscular discomfort
- ❏ Vision problems
- ❏ Hearing problems
- ❏ Digestive issues
- ❏ Past or recent injury
- ❏ Breathing problems (especially short-snouted dogs like Pugs and Bulldogs)

Instinctual: Different dogs have different needs. Does your dog get the opportunity to participate in rewarding behaviors? Dogs can have obsessions (be Hyper-Focused) when they don't have jobs or if their instinctual needs are not met. If you know your dog's breed, do an internet search for what the dog was bred for. You may find that introducing a certain behavior in a healthy manner could satisfy her need.

- ❏ Fetching/retrieving (a ball, not the cat)
- ❏ Chasing (playfully with another dog, not the cat)
- ❏ Tearing (a plush toy, not the cat)
- ❏ Pulling and tugging (a rope toy, not the cat... are you sensing a theme here?)
- ❏ Chewing (rubbery toys)
- ❏ Gnawing (bone, hardwood, antlers, etc.)
- ❏ Herding

- ❏ Nose work
- ❏ Guarding
- ❏ Digging

Exercise: Is your dog high-strung? Start with exercise. (Even little dogs need walks.)

- ❏ Walking/Running
- ❏ Play
- ❏ Swimming
- ❏ Joring (pulling)
- ❏ Agility

Mental Stimulation: Does your dog get to do interesting things?

- ❏ Puzzle toys, stuffed Kongs™, treat balls, etc.
- ❏ Agility training
- ❏ Obedience training
- ❏ New smells
- ❏ New places
- ❏ Car rides

Social Stimulation: How interesting is your dog's world?

- ❏ Other dogs (if your dog is dog-friendly)
- ❏ People (if your dog is people-friendly)

Affection: Does your dog feel loved?

- ❏ "Good gurrrl!"
- ❏ Belly rubs, chin scratches, whatever your dog enjoys

2. Which of these items will I start with to see if my dog's behavior changes without need for any further "training"?

_____

_____

_____

Takeaway
Consideration must be given to the physical, mental, instinctual, intellectual and emotional health and wellness of the dog before assuming the dog needs behavior modification.

Chapter 5: Energy-Obedient Over Behavior-Obedient

If you walked away from this workbook having learned only one thing, my hope is it might be this: managing energy level (intensity) is the key to managing behavior. Many of us are quick to reward our dogs for obedience. What if that paradigm were to change?

Yes, your dog may sit when you ask her to. She also may be a hair trigger away from chasing a squirrel, stealing your sandwich, hiding under the bed or biting. I would trade away obedience for a calm energy state any day. Sitting *may* be an indicator of a calm dog, but there is a difference between "excited obedient" and "calm obedient". "Excited obedient" is like tapping the pause button on the TV remote whereas "calm obedient" is more like pressing stop.

Too Much
When you arrive home and your dog greets you, maybe she is happy and excited - too excited - more like hyperactive. Is she jumping or spinning? Does she pee on the floor from excitement? She wants your attention and affection, badly. "Mommy's home!" Is there any criteria for her being able to interact with you? Maybe you ask for a sit, but she launches right back to hyperactive a split second later. What would it look like to ask for some self control, so that you might interact with her in a calmer, safer manner? It may involve restraint on your part. Enter the house, and wait. When the hyperactivity fades, give her calm affection and attention.

The first time you try this, she might be annoyed or frustrated. She might even be more hyperactive than usual. "Eeeeeeesy, girrrrl." Slow and deliberate. She may get frustrated and walk away. That's fine. When she comes back, is she calmer? If so, calmly reward her with your affection and engagement. If not, keep waiting. Can you (and the rest of your family *and your guests*) change the greeting ritual such that calmness is always a prerequisite of affection? She may always feel super-excited when you get home, but it won't take long before she learns that there is an expectation that must be met for her to receive the reward of interaction.

Not Enough
Interestingly enough, a similar approach may help with a shy or timid dog with one big difference: the reward is for an *increase* in engagement and energy rather than a decrease. When you arrive home, enter quietly and respectfully. If your dog isn't the type to greet you at the door, go to the room she is in and sit on the floor or a low chair at a distance that requires her to move at least a little bit to receive affection. Calmly encourage any movement towards you. To receive physical affection, all she needs to do is to make this small journey. If your dog is food motivated, you can up the reward by giving treats when she enters your personal space.

This may sound easy, but it is not what most of us do with shy dogs. We come home, go right to the dog and pet her or pick her up (depending on her size). We are the invasive one, unlike the example above. The dog doesn't have a choice about receiving affection. She probably likes affection, but on her terms. Maybe, with some restraint and patience on our part, we can expand her terms; we can increase the size of her comfort zone to include approaching people.

There are two different ways to expand this exercise. First, you can increase the distance between yourself and the dog, working you way towards whatever location you would like her to greet you (maybe it is right by the front door, maybe someplace else), so instead of sitting near her, sit farther and farther away, even in another room, encouraging more movement. The second way to expand this exercise is to include other people. Can you ask your friend to follow your lead when entering the house? Two calm people sit and wait for the dog to initiate the meeting. If she chooses not to initiate, don't push it. If she feels that she has the option, the next time her bravery might surprise you.

Empathy: Energy is Contagious
Dogs, like children, are very susceptible to the emotional energy of others in the room. For those of you with multiple dogs, I would imagine you've seen one dog's behavior transfer to another. When Olive barks, Tickle starts barking even if she has no idea what Olive is interested in. For those of you with multiple children, I would guess you've seen the same thing happen (the energy transfer, not the barking, I hope). Even as adults, many of us are susceptible to this. Have you ever received a phone call from a friend or family member who is anxious or frantic and so you start to feel anxious or frantic before you even know what is bothering the other person? This is a part of empathy. You might think of empathy as something related primarily to sadness, but the definition applies to all feelings: empathy is "the ability to share someone else's feelings."

Another aspect of this is emotional violence. If a parent were to yell at an older child while a younger child was in the room, the younger child will likely experience it as if they were being yelled at. While adults can (sometimes) differentiate, children by and large cannot. Similarly, a fight between spouses can be traumatic for the kids, and in the same vein, dogs may be adversely affected by negative emotional energy between humans. If your family is experiencing trauma, there is a good chance the dog is as well.

Clarifying What We Want
When I'm relaxing, I'd like my dogs to be relaxing too. That's not always what happens. Sometimes, the dogs want to chase each other and wrestle in the house (which is far from relaxing for me). If I only ask them to sit, they will be back at it a moment later. I want to engage with them where my intent is to convey that calmness is what I'm looking for. If they sit, fine. I don't really care. If they lie down, great, but still not the goal. The goal is for them to understand, "Daddy says it's time to chill. I can choose *what* I'm doing, but Daddy is being very clear about *how* he wants me to do it." Part of this is the style of conversation we have with the dog; the other part comes from our demeanor and our goal being "energy obedient" instead of "behavior obedient".

Treats For "Nothing"
Here is one last version of this concept: treat your dog for relaxing. When you dog is calmly lying on her bed, walk over, lean down and give her a treat for "doing" *nothing*. "You're being a good girl right now," is the message you are giving her. "Relaxed is good. I approve of your calm, balanced energy state."

Exercise 5: Energy-Obedient Over Behavior-Obedient

1. Congratulations! You have already read the instructions for this first part of the exercise near the beginning of this chapter. Now it is time to try for yourself.

    a. For dogs with more *invasive* energy, follow the example in the section "Too Much."

    b. For dogs with more *avoidant* energy, follow the example in the section "Not Enough."

2. Figure out how to consistently be "the Zen master of greeting *your* dog."

    Notice how different your behavior and demeanor was compared to how you might have greeted her yesterday. If you had positive results doing this exercise, what might you remind yourself each time you enter to create *your* habituation so that your dog has the opportunity to do the same? For example: "Take a deep breath," "Relax," "Be patient," "Don't give in to her energy," "I can be restrained for the emotional health of my dog," etc.?

    _____

3. Did you notice anything different about your dog's body language during the exercise?
   Hint: "Take her T-E-M-P" (Tail, Eyes/Ears, Mouth, Posture)

    _____

    _____

    _____

4. Bonus exercise for balanced or higher-energy dogs:

    Show your dog that you are holding a high value treat, such as a piece of hot dog. Let her smell it in your hand. Stand in front of her and ask her to sit. Don't give her the treat. Wait to see how long it takes her to fully relax without prompting. If she gets up, put her back in the sit. Let her try to figure out what you want. She may first go in the other direction: pawing at your hand, jumping, barking, etc. Be patient: your calmness will help her find her calmness. The energy shift down could be that her tail stops wagging, she shifts to a more relaxed sit, a softening of her eyes or just a calmness. When you see the shift, reward her with the treat and a calm, reassuring "good girl." The "conversation" is now over and she will likely be more relaxed than if you had just rewarded for the sit. As she learns that sit *and* being calm is what will earn the treat, her downshift of energy will become a learned and easily repeatable behavior.

Takeaway
Traditional obedience classes look for behavior as the indicator of success. We can choose to look at energy level as that indicator, with calm and attentive being the gold standard of obedience.

Chapter 6: Our Role In The Relationship

Being in harmony with any approach taken with your dog is of the utmost importance. I once watched a trainer put a prong collar on a twelve pound Maltese/Shih Tzu mix. There was no way on Earth that the owner, a petite woman in her 60's, was going to jerk and pull her little cuddle bunny into obedience. Might it have worked to get the dog to sit, stay and heel? Maybe, but it didn't work at all for the owner.

On the flip side, an owner who had a non-food motivated Akita found that a prong collar and a commanding demeanor was exactly what her dog needed. With his thick fur coat, she felt it very unlikely that she was doing any harm to the dog, and he was responsive and easy-going when she "played alpha dog" in the relationship. While I am not personally a fan of prong collars, if she felt comfortable, wasn't hurting the dog, got consistent results, and the dog seemed unbothered by it, who am I to tell her what she is doing is "wrong"?

If your interaction style is in conflict with what kind of pet parent you want to be, I doubt you'll maintain it. Either your opinion of your behavior or the behavior itself must change, or having a dog will eternally stress you out. Do what works for you.

Nurture, Guidance & Limits
Parenting is the continually-changing balance between loving our children, teaching our children and keeping them safe. For example, a child who is only loved won't know how to make his or her way in the world or how to stay out of danger. A child raised in a world of limits may stay safe but may not feel loved or know how to think for him or herself. This paradigm translates very well to dogs.

"Yay! It's Mommy!" Vs. "Hi Mom!" Vs. "Yes, Mother"
We can split "pet parenting" into three styles:
1. Mommy/Daddy
2. Mom/Dad
3. Mother/Father

I believe *there is a time and a place for each style in every human/canine relationship*. Have you ever seen a dog's energy level change when the husband hands the leash to the wife, or vice versa? When a dog knows what is expected of it, it knows what mindset to get into. The dog doesn't have to guess. If we as pet parents can show our dogs what kind of energy we're looking for, or if we can give them an energy state to model, it allows them to focus on the activity at hand, be it a walk, play, obedience, cuddling or whatever else.

Let's look at each parenting style one by one.

Mommy/Daddy
- In order of importance: nurture, possibly some guidance, probably few or no limits
- Emotionally driven
- Treating the dog like a baby
- Out of proportion, it may be more for you than for the dog (selfish)
- Extremely common with owners of small/toy breeds
- The dog may be suffering in a directionless, unstructured world, and you may be ruled by a bratty, mannerless dog

Mom/Dad
- In order of importance: guidance, then nurture and limits
- Intellectually driven
- Less exciting than being Mommy, less structured than being Mother
- Ask the dog to work for rewards. It will have more value, build trust and strengthen the relationship. Asking a dog to sit before giving affection is not mean.
- Want the dog's world to expand so that the dog can be challenged and grow.

Mother/Father
- In order of importance: limits, then guidance, then nurture
- Safety driven
- Be benevolent, even when reprimanding. *There is no need for meanness, ever.* Beware of becoming a tyrant: one who rules over the dog through obedience, fear and punishment. If you have a short temper, there is great potential for emotionally harming your dog, so get it under control.
- Some behaviors are not acceptable, such as chasing the cat or jumping up on young children. Your communication with the dog does not have to be punitive, but it does need to be decisive, consistent and effective, so no one gets hurt.

A consistent situational pattern of pet parenting style will create structure, which dogs thrive on. For example:
- Mommy/Daddy: cuddling on the couch or bed
- Mommy/Daddy: playing in the backyard, safe and fenced in
- Mom/Dad: everyday around the house
- Mom/Dad: on walks around the neighborhood
- Mother/Father: doorbell rings unexpectedly
- Mother/Father: an unfamiliar barking dog passes too close

"But I Want To Be Mommy All The Time!"
That is of course your choice, and, there may be consequences. Giving affection is the same as saying, "I approve of what you are doing." Do you always mean to be saying that? Affection given at the wrong time can reinforce unwanted behaviors. "Isn't it cute how she jumps up and wants to lick your face?" Yes, it's adorable, until she does it to a stranger and accidentally catches her tooth on their lip, and you get sued. Sometimes parents need to be stern and firm with their kids for their own safety. With dogs the same is also true.

Deliberate, Compassionate & Consistent
If you were terrified or raging, what kind of energy would help to bring *you* back to reality? How about a friend or parent with your well-being in mind, with a plan to calm things down, who would not be swayed by your continued extreme behavior? That is Deliberate, Compassionate and Consistent.

What is not part of Deliberate, Compassionate and Consistent? Being anxious, distracted, punitive, unsure, arbitrary, timid, contemptuous, exasperated, etc.. Your dog can feed off of this negative energy just as easily as off of your calmness. Can you be the person your dog needs you to be? I'll bet you can. And, while it may take some work and some practice, if your intent is to be Deliberate, Compassionate and Consistent, you are already halfway there.

Deliberate, Compassionate and Consistent: this is *your* Balance, *your* center. You are a strong, loving, knowledgeable leader - firm but fair - guiding your dog through the world.

Appropriate Use Of Volume
It is possible to increase volume without changing parenting style. You can be loud and nurturing at the same time. How would you praise a toddler who went down a slide by himself at the playground for the first time? "What a GOOD BOY! I'm SOOO proud of you!" The same thing can be effective with your dog. Remember, she's about as evolved as a 2½ year old child. Often, if I give a command with just a little more volume (not more anger), I get a more immediate and enthusiastic response from the dog.

A Note About Embarrassment (on our part)
Avoiding embarrassment has its roots in fight or flight. "If I am seen as bad or wrong or stupid, people will look down on me or even shun me. And if that happens enough, I might die alone! I must avoid embarrassment!" That is the voice of fear. It can be a strong motivator. Often, fear of embarrassment leads to avoidant behavior. If we avoid working on the things that embarrass us, we will never make any improvement and they will remain as sources of embarrassment into the future. If you are willing to be uncomfortable in the short term as you work on your dog's behavior, you can set up the long term to be less embarrassing. So accept the fact that someone might see your dog jump or pull or bark: breathe, and know that the work you put in now will make the future much more bearable.

Exercise 6: Our Role in the Relationship

1. My tendency is to lean towards (check one):

    ❏ Nurture
    ❏ Guidance
    ❏ Limits

2. My dog could probably benefit from more (check one or more):

    ❏ Nurture
    ❏ Guidance
    ❏ Limits

3. Situations where being Mommy/Daddy feels most appropriate and would be helpful for my dog:

    _____
    _____
    _____
    _____

4. Situations where being Mom/Dad feels most appropriate and would be helpful for my dog:

    _____
    _____
    _____
    _____

5. Situations where being Mother/Father feels most appropriate and would be helpful for my dog:

    _____
    _____
    _____
    _____

6. The relationship with my dog could benefit most from my being more (check any that apply):

    ❏ Deliberate
    ❏ Compassionate
    ❏ Consistent

7. A situation when my embarrassment might cause me to avoid acting in the best interest of my dog is when he/she:

    _____

    and my response is to:

    _____.

    In the future, I will commit to

    _____instead.

Takeaway

We have an important role to play in the relationship with our dog. While our style may fluctuate from more gentle to more balanced to more stern, (from Mommy to Mom to Mother) our responsibility is to nurture, guide and protect our dog. Being Deliberate, Compassionate and Consistent is a great way to accomplish this.

Chapter 7: Confidence - Dogs That Make Good Decisions

How would you rate your dog at making good decisions? An overly confident dog will often act quickly but what they choose to do may or may not be desirable or safe. A more timid dog may shut down and try to avoid deciding. A balanced dog in the middle will likely experiment in order to figure out what the best path forward might be, or they may look to you for guidance. Confidence comes from making decisions that result in positive outcomes. A positive outcome may mean any number of things: a scary thing goes away, the dog gets a treat or receives affection, etc. Hopefully we are all looking for some version of the same thing: a dog that makes good decisions.

What are good decisions? First (hopefully), they are decisions where the dog remains safe and those around the dog also remain safe. And second, they are decisions that you as the owner decide are good decisions. What do I mean by that? If, for example, you want a watch dog that barks when a stranger approaches, then you are more likely to agree and reward the decision to bark. If on the other hand you want a dog that greets strangers with affection, barking would be considered undesirable.

Overly confident dogs often decide on their own or with little regard for your wishes. If barking makes a stranger go away and that is what *they* want (to create distance from the stranger), then the dog will likely bark. Another variation could be a dog that decides it wants to jump up to lick people's faces. The dog wants to do that, but you may not want the dog to do that. Often, these dogs have not been shown limits. Too much confidence results in a dog that is disobedient and possibly dangerous.

Timid or fearful dogs may lack experience making decisions or have a poor track record of positive results from decision making. An example of the former would be a dog that was never properly socialized with other dogs that is now scared of other dogs. An example of the latter would be a dog that tried to socialize with other dogs but was attacked. Both dogs are afraid but for different reasons, whether it is "I don't know what to do," or "I don't want that to happen again." Often, owners fail to offer guidance and instead over-nurture, resulting in dogs that remain fearful.

Dogs gain confidence from making decisions that result in positive outcomes.
If you want to tame an unruly or overconfident dog, the negative consequences of bad decisions may need to increase. If you want to empower a timid or shy dog, the positive consequences of good decisions may need to increase. For a dog that is balanced (neither overconfident nor timid), good decision making can be taught by rewarding what you want and correcting what you don't, guiding the dog towards the decision you want it to make. Repetition is reinforcing: the more often the dog is able to make a good decision when presented with a specific situation, the more confident the dog will become in that situation.

Example #1: Copper, the bossy dog
Copper does whatever she wants, including stealing food from the dinner table. The positive consequence is getting the food. The (barely) negative consequence is her owner saying "bad dog" half-heartedly. If we change the balance of good to bad, she will in all likelihood start to make better decisions. The next time she tries stealing food, her owner does something unpleasant at the exact

moment when Copper starts to lift her nose up to the table, such as loudly and sharply saying "NO!" or stomping their foot, then stands up and herds her (Chapter 12) to the other side of the room or to her bed. If Copper tries to come back to the table, she is herded, again and again if necessary, until she decides not to try again. At the end of the meal, Copper's owner rewards her by bringing a piece of food over to her. The new message: "I get food over here, not when I steal it. I will decide to hang out over here when my owner is eating because that is how I will get a treat."

Where we often go wrong with bossy dogs: lack of consistency, lack of follow-through, laziness

Example #2: Zoey, the fearful dog
Zoey is afraid of the dishwasher. Hiding in her crate when the dishwasher is on creates two positive consequences: first, it creates distance (which feels safe), and second, her owner comes in and pets her and tells her "It's okay, sweetie," (another reinforcer to continue hiding). If instead, her owner placed extremely high value treats (see Chapter 11) at first right in front of Zoey, and then after she took them, a few inches away but still inside the crate, then right outside the crate, then a foot outside the crate... each time gently praising Zoey's decision to venture out (saying "goooooooood girrrrrrrl!" calmly and supportively), the balance of negative to positive consequences might tip towards venturing out. The new message: "I get treats *and* praise when I choose to leave the crate while the dishwasher is on... *and* I don't have to go all the way to the dishwasher if I don't want, so it feels safe too!" We add no negative consequences; we just increase the positive. Be aware, with fearful dogs, even looking towards you when the dishwasher is on might be scary. Zoey should be rewarded for every decision she makes that is *in any way a step in the right direction*.

Where we often go wrong with timid dogs: forcing them to do things that put them over-threshold, impatience, over-nurturing

Example #3: Daisy, the balanced dog
Daisy is good-natured and reasonably obedient. She trusts her owner but can be tentative in new situations. Also, she can be a little too friendly with other leashed dogs and sometimes approaches dogs who do not want to be approached. Daisy cares about her owner's reaction, so if her owner is observant and engaged, Daisy has the potential to become a well-balanced, confident dog. When she encounters something unknown but safe such as a dragonfly, her owner can be guiding and nurturing by "giving permission" to investigate, maybe by saying "It's okay, Daisy" in an encouraging tone. When she shows interest in something unknown and unsafe, such as pulling towards a stranger who is approaching on a bicycle, a combination of guidance and limits from her owner will be more appropriate: saying "uh-uh!" and applying firm but gentle tension to the leash until Daisy chooses to change direction, at which point the tension is released.

Where we often go wrong with balanced dogs: letting them do whatever they want because they are "good dogs", waiting until they are already in trouble so our suggestion of what we want instead becomes a punishment for what they already did

Example #4: Muffin, the terrified aggressive dog
Muffin pulls, lunges and bites when she meets strange people and strange dogs, especially if they are in her home. She goes Over Threshold almost immediately and maintains that intensity until whatever is

scaring her is gone. Like Zoey, Muffin found a strategy to deal with her fear (deciding to bite, lunge and bark) that produces positive results: her owners pick her up and carry her into another room (resulting in the desired effect of creating distance). Unfortunately, Muffin's decision is neither safe nor desired by her owner. In this situation, Muffin needs to learn that her decision to bite, pull and lunge is undesirable, but since she is already terrified, anything too punitive or aversive may push her even farther over the edge. We need to get Muffin to a place where she chooses to try something new.

Here is one way we might accomplish this. We set up a gate between two adjacent rooms, one of which has a door to the outside. Let's call that room the living room and the other room we will call the kitchen. The owner has Muffin leashed in the living room. Then we have someone whom Muffin is not comfortable around knock on the door and then enter the living room. Muffin begins to bark and lunge. The owner moves Muffin to the kitchen and closes the gate but remains close to the gate and drops the leash. We allow Muffin to continue whatever she is doing, but we look to reward any more positive choice she makes. If she pauses her lunging, the owner says "Gooooooood girrrrrrrl!" encouragingly and gives her a high-value treat. If Muffin turns and looks towards the kitchen, same thing. Anything she does that is an improvement gets rewarded. Any return to unwanted behavior is ignored.

Where we often go wrong with terrified aggressive dogs: punishing them while they are terrified, moving too fast and expecting that we can "fix" them on our timeline not theirs, being embarrassed and never addressing their behavior.

Exercise 7: Confidence - Dogs That Make Good Decisions

1. What are some situations in which your dog makes poor decisions?

   _____

   _____

   _____

   _____

2. My dog needs more (circle one):

   Encouragement to build confidence   Discouragement to reduce overconfidence

3. How does that translate to Nurture, Guidance and Limits (from Chapter 6)?
   My dog needs (circle one):

   More nurture and guidance   More guidance and limits

Takeaway

A dog who is given the opportunity to make a decision and then receives new feedback about that decision is a dog who is learning. Some dogs may need encouragement and a safe environment in which to practice decision-making, while other dogs may need more of our feedback when their decisions result in unsafe or unwanted consequences.

Chapter 8: Become a Dog Detective (Situation-Feeling-Behavior)

Imagine if you will, that dogs file their memories away like pictures in an album. The pictures show *situations*, such as seeing a strange man in a black hat approaching. Attached to each picture is an emotion or *feeling*: how does the dog *feel* about a strange man in a black hat approaching? And when the dog feels this emotion, what is the dog's corresponding *behavior*?

Situation predicts Feeling, and Feeling predicts Behavior.

Situation → **Feeling** → **Behavior**

People often like to know *why* something has happened, but with dogs (especially fostered and rescued dogs) we may never know the backstory or the reason the dog created the picture. That's fine. Understanding *what* the picture contains is the important part. Did a man in a black hat yell at your dog, beat your dog, yell at another dog, yell at his kids, beat his kids, pass out drunk, kick a garbage can, etc.? It doesn't really matter. *Something* scary happened, and your dog connects fear to men *plus* black hats. When a man isn't wearing the hat, there's no problem; when he is, your dog freaks out. When a woman wears a black hat it is okay; man in a black hat: terror.

Past interpretations are the narratives we may tell ourselves based on observation, intuition and guesswork. If you tell me that you believe a man in a black hat beat your rescued dog in her previous home because she cowers in fear when she sees a man in a black hat, I won't tell you that you are wrong; obviously I have no way of knowing either. If you have the details of the situation correctly identified, that is enough to allow rehabilitation or reconditioning to progress; the why, for our purposes, is irrelevant.

If we can connect the situation to a different feeling, we will also be connecting it to a different behavior. But first, we need to recognize the picture. Here are a few examples with past interpretations included...

Situation		Past Interpretation		Feeling		Behavior
Man in black hat approaches	→	a man in a black hat once yelled at us	→	scared	→	try to hide
Man in no hat approaches	→	I have no negative data on hatless men	→	curious	→	sniff
Woman in black hat approaches	→	I have no negative data on women in black hats	→	curious	→	sniff
Man in white hat approaches	→	I have no negative data on men in white hats	→	curious	→	sniff
Daddy in a black hat approaches	→	I know Daddy well enough to not care if he's wearing a black hat	→	happy	→	lick Daddy's face

| Man in black hat stays over there | → | I'm okay right now... | → | cautious | → | watchful |

...but realize that the past interpretations are basically guesses. When we remove the past interpretations, the pictures become much clearer (as do the conclusions):

Situation		Feeling		Behavior
Man in black hat approaches	→	scared	→	try to hide
Man in no hat approaches	→	curious	→	sniff
Woman in black hat approaches	→	curious	→	sniff
Man in white hat approaches	→	curious	→	sniff
Daddy in a black hat approaches	→	happy	→	lick his face
Man in black hat stays over there	→	cautious	→	watchful

My dog is scared and tries to hide when:
1. a man
2. wears a hat
3. it is a black hat
4. the man is not Daddy
5. he approaches

Do we have *all* of the important details that trigger the emotional response? Have we painted the right picture? All 5 conditions of the situation must be met for the feeling to be "scared" and the behavior to be "try to hide."

Let's say we were trying to figure out the specific picture that results in your dog lunging and barking. It seems to be related to her meeting other dogs, but her behavior isn't predictable; sometimes she's fine and other times she lunges and barks. Below, we will test some variables in the situation so that we can predict her behavior with more accuracy:

Situation		Feeling		Behavior
Dog I know approaches	→	happy	→	tail wags
Small dog I don't know approaches	→	happy	→	tail wags
Large dark-colored dog I don't know approaches	→	unsure / suspicious	→	tail up, stops wagging

Situation		Feeling		Behavior
Large light-colored dog I don't know approaches	→	happy	→	tail wags
Large light-colored dog I don't know runs towards me	→	happy	→	tail wags
Large dark-colored dog I don't know runs towards me	→	defensive / territorial	→	tail up, lunging & barking
Small dark-colored dog I don't know runs towards me	→	happy	→	tail wags

We can conclude that your dog will lunge and bark when all of the following criteria is met:
1. a strange dog
2. that is large
3. and dark in color
4. approaches
5. quickly

Here's another one:

Situation		Feeling		Behavior
Maltese, Bichon, Min Pin, Rat Terrier or Pomeranian approaches	→	happy	→	tail wags
Light-colored Chihuahua approaches	→	defensive / territorial	→	tail up, lunging & barking
Dark-colored Chihuahua approaches	→	defensive / territorial	→	tail up, lunging & barking
Light-colored Chihuahua stays over there	→	defensive / territorial	→	tail up, lunging & barking
Dark-colored Chihuahua stays over there	→	defensive / territorial	→	tail up, lunging & barking

That one was easy: your dog hates chihuahuas.

A very important variable to be aware of is your own presence. Does your dog feel and behave in the same manner if someone else is holding the leash, or if she is by herself? *You* may be part of the situation.

I worked with a woman whose dog was terrified of going through portals (doorways, gates, etc). After some trial and error, she discovered that her dog was afraid of going through portals *alone*. When she leashed her dog and walked confidently through a doorway ahead of her dog, her dog didn't even seem to notice the door frame: "When mom is here to lead the way, I am not afraid." So what the woman learned was that [doorways + alone → fear → cower and resist movement], but [doorways + mom + leash → fine → walk through].

Exercise 8: Become a Dog Detective (Situation-Feeling-Behavior)

1. What is a situation in which you would like your dog to behave in a different manner?

   _____

2. What behavior are you getting now?

   _____

3. Through body language (or anything else you have learned), can you make an educated guess as to how your dog is feeling?

   _____

4. Fill in the first row of the table below using your answers from questions 1-3.

5. Now, what variables might you want to consider to make sure you have an accurate picture of the situation that produces the feeling that produces the behavior? What can you test to make sure you have the right criteria such that you are able to consistently predict the response? For example: you might have a dog who hates every chihuahua she meets when you walk her on leash. But what if your spouse is walking her? There is a very important piece of information gathered if *you* are a criteria that predicts the behavior. Think of as many variables to the situation as you can and test them out. Record your results, starting in row 2. If you need more room, grab a piece of lined paper and keep going with the variables until you feel confident that you have the situation clearly defined.

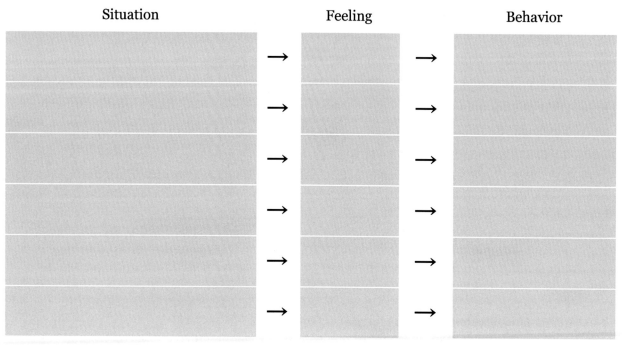

Takeaway
Situation, feeling, and behavior are often linked in a dog's mind. When we are very clear on the criteria that makes up the situation, we are much more likely to be solving the right problem.

Chapter 9: The Debate Over "Positive Reinforcement" & "Pack Leader"

There is usually more than one way to skin a cat, or in this case, to train a dog. Many trainers fall into one of two categories:

1. Positive Reinforcement-Based Training: sometimes called "Positive Only" or "Positive Training"
or
2. Pack Leader or Dominance Theory, sometimes called "Alpha Dog" or "Aversive Training"

The language is misleading: positive in the technical sense here doesn't mean "good," it means "the addition of." Pack Leader may rely on concepts of dominance and punishment, yet the word punishment has a more negative connotation in its common use than it does scientifically. Punishment does not have to involve physical or emotional harm. It just needs to serve to reduce the likelihood of the dog repeating the behavior.

Reinforcement aims to increase a desirable behavior.
Punishment aims to decrease an undesirable behavior.

They both come from a system called *operant conditioning*:

The Four Quadrants of Operant Conditioning

Positive (additive) Reinforcement: R+	**Positive (additive) Punishment:** P+
Reward: Treats, praise or affection	**Correction**: The addition of something aversive or unpleasant
Negative (subtractive) Reinforcement: R-	**Negative (subtractive) Punishment:** P-
Relief: Removing discomfort or ending a disagreement*	**Denial**: Taking a toy or freedom away

*More on disagreements in Chapter 12

A technique I have seen many "positive" trainers use is to stop moving forward when the dog starts pulling on the leash. Is this removing freedom (negative punishment) or introducing resistance (positive punishment)? I believe most people would not regard this as cruel, yet it could be defined as punishment. In my mind, the only difference is semantics. I doubt the dog knows, or cares.

I think many of us would, in concept, prefer to lean towards reward-based interactions with our dog. There's no question that it is more fun to give a treat than to say "no". And, at the same time, if my dog is Over Threshold and in danger of hurting herself or someone else, I'll use whatever humane method is going to get her out of that situation. A punish-*ment* does not need to be punish-*ing*.

There is an acronym that is gaining some exposure that I believe to be more accurate than the term "positive": "LIMA", which stands for Least Intrusive Minimally Aversive. I am a big fan of this language. The idea is to look to utilize the least invasive and most reinforcing technique first - then if that is unsuccessful, try the next most humane and compassionate technique until you find what works.

Can you imagine raising a human toddler using a reward-only system? I doubt it. The kid would be completely spoiled and get treated for *everything*. Don't want Sally to run into the street? "If you stay on the sidewalk I'll give you a popsicle, Honey." Don't want her hitting her baby brother? "How about a brownie?" Eventually, the child will want bigger and better rewards, like a new cell phone or a car. Sometimes it's okay *and not cruel* to say "no".

Where To Start?
Low-confidence or fearful dogs may react poorly to punishment. Over-confident dogs may require some correction when bribery (reward) doesn't offer enough incentive to stop an unwanted behavior. The same technique will be more effective with some dogs than with others. What is aversive for some dogs is just communication for other dogs: 'Dog A' may be scared when you say "no" while 'Dog B' may simply take it at face value: "Oh. My owner would prefer me to stop counter-surfing." My advice to you? Take the LIMA approach. Start with positive reinforcement. If that is unsuccessful, try the next most humane and compassionate technique until you find what works. If you feel like you are punishing your dog; if your dog seems scared of what you are doing: stop, back up, and rethink your approach.

Exercise 9: Positive & Negative, Reward & Punishment

1. In the left column, list some things you already do to modify your dog's behavior. For example: giving treats for "sit", tugging on the leash when she stops too long to sniff, ignoring her when she's jumping up, etc.

2. In the right column, write whether you see this as positive reinforcement (reward), negative reinforcement (relief), positive punishment (correction) or negative punishment (denial).

Operation (What *you* do to correct a behavior)	Quadrant

3. Some dogs are very treat-motivated, while other dogs actually do better by avoiding what they feel are negative consequences. Do you find any of the quadrants to be more effective than others *with your dog*?

   _____

4. Do you find any of these quadrants to be more your *style* than the others?

   _____

5. What quadrant(s) did your parents use raising you, and how?
   (If this is too personal, do it in your head. I included it so you might consider what it is like being on the receiving end of different operant strategies.)

Operation (What Mom or Dad did to correct *your* behavior)	Quadrant

Takeaway

The language can be deceiving. "Positive Only" sounds great but is not entirely accurate. The technical and common usage of these words is not identical. Sometimes we want to encourage more of a behavior, and reinforcement will often assist in that. At other times, we may want to discourage a behavior, and "punishment" (again, the technical term) may assist us in doing so.

Chapter 10: Not Carrot or Stick, Carrot *and* Stick

So what is a real-world take away from the Positive Reinforcement/Pack Leader debate? Trainers on both sides get results and build careers based on their successes. Also, they seem to be very polarized: "My way is the only way and the other way is ineffective/cruel/not based on science/etc." Why can't we meet in the middle? We can.

I'll sum it up in five words: "Not that, this. Good dog!"

Correct, Request, Reward
If "punishment" reduces an unwanted behavior and "reinforcement" increases a desired behavior, why not double down and do both? I'll give you an example.

Momo is very happy when I get home and let him out of his crate. If I let him out and immediately walk away he will follow me and usually be a little mouthy, gently taking my hand or the tail of my shirt in his mouth. He knows that when I snap my fingers, it means I do not like what he is doing, but it also means I am about to give a command, so I snap my fingers ("Momo, don't do 'that'") and he will stop mouthing. Then I request a sit ("How about doing 'this'?"), which he does. Now it's time for "good boy" and some head rubs (reward).

Similarly, sometimes Momo will stand at the fence and bark at a dog passing by. If I only correct him, ("Cut it out!") what is he supposed to do, just stand there and not bark? I doubt that would work. So it's Correct, Request, Reward. "Momo, uh-uh!" to get his attention (the snap wouldn't be loud enough from across the yard), then my hand signal for "touch" (Chapter 17) which he knows means he will get a treat, and I've got Momo running to me for his reward.

Offering reinforcement or punishment for behaviors (operant conditioning from the previous chapter) is one of the simpler approaches to behavior modification. It takes for granted that your dog is listening and somewhat responsive. If your dog is Over Threshold (she has entered The Ring Of Fire), she may need some of the concepts in the chapters that follow.

Exercise 10: Carrot & Stick

1. Are there things your dog does, such as counter surfing or chewing on your slipper, that could use some attention? Instead of just saying "no", Correct, Request and Reward. List behaviors that may have been corrected before where now you could utilize all three steps:

Behavior	Correction	Request	Reward
Ex: counter surfing	"Uh-uh!" or snap	"Come!"	Treat and "Good Girl!"

Takeaway
"Not that. This. Good dog!"

Chapter 11: The Power of Positivity

The Clicker
One of the most popular training tools these days is the clicker. The dog performs a task, (sit, for example) and the trainer clicks and then gives the dog a treat. The click becomes the precursor to reward. But this clicker, this marking device, has other uses besides confirmation of a behavior well done.

Counter-Conditioning: Breaking The Connection Between Situation, Feeling, & Behavior
Once the connection between click and reward has been established with the dog (over a few days or weeks, not a few minutes), the clicker can perform a very different function. Since the dog is used to receiving a treat after hearing the click, the click is a welcome, happy sound. What would happen if you clicked not as a confirmation of behavior, but as a summoning of happiness? Here is an example:

Let's say you are trying to improve your dog's reactivity to men in black hats. A common sense approach would be to give the dog a treat after not pulling on the leash when passing a black-hatted man. That makes sense. But the counter-conditioning approach would be to click and treat as soon as your dog sees the man. Essentially, you are introducing a reward before your dog reacts. So instead of processing the picture like this...

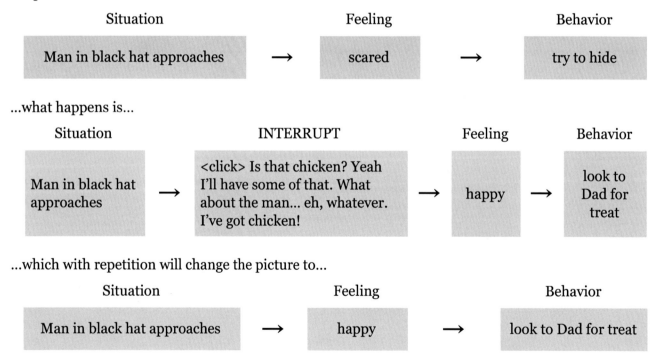

Clowns & Chocolate
I'll paint a similar picture using people. I'm going to use a ridiculous example so that maybe it is more memorable. Let's say you're afraid of clowns. Every time you see a clown you feel very nervous and want to run the other way. As your friend, we walk together a few nights a week for exercise. One night, you and I are walking together and we see a clown walking in our direction. Upon noticing the clown, I reach into my pocket and pull out two chocolate bars. "Hey, a clown!" I exclaim happily and hand you a chocolate bar. You ask me why I did that. "Well, when I was growing up, my dad would get us chocolate bars when we went to the circus. So whenever I see a clown (or an elephant or a guy on stilts), I think of chocolate. Seeing the clown reminded me that I just happened to have chocolate in my pocket."

If this happened only once, it might not make any difference. But if every time we went walking we saw a clown and I gave you a chocolate bar, it wouldn't be long before you began expecting a chocolate bar when we saw a clown. Now you may still be afraid of clowns, but when walking with me, clowns = chocolate and nothing bad ever happens. A novel response to break an old memory.

Counter-conditioning can be used to reprogram a number of different pictures. When your dog hears the mailman on the front porch, how would she react if you scattered food on the floor at that exact moment? If your dog is afraid of thunder, how would she respond to getting high value treats with each burst? The doorbell and thunder could be reprogrammed as positive experiences. The doorbell rings, you click and say "treat!" and the dog gets to scour the floor for kibble. Thunder sounds <click> and the dog gets a piece of hot dog. (If the dog is absolutely terrified, she may not take the treat. Still, the introduction of the positive marker may eventually take hold.)

Lose the Clicker
The clicker is used because it is cheap, simple and effective. But most of us don't want to carry a clicker around with us for the rest of our dog's life. And, if we're not ready to use it at the perfect moment, it becomes useless. So what can we use that doesn't require holding a device in our hands all the time? Our voice. Using the same quick tone and delivery can produce similar results. Simply say "Treat!" in a pleasant, deliberate, optimistic Daddy-voice, followed by the treat.

Projecting Positive Emotion
Just as in the clown story, we can express joy (or calm or any other feeling) with our voice. When you see your dog notice another dog up ahead, *how* you say what you say is what is important here. Project how you want the dog to feel. "Look at the cute doggie. Is it a Schnauzer or a Scottie? Very cute. You like little dogs, don't you? Passing dogs in the park is delightful." - a constant stream of pleasant, optimistic Daddy-speak. It doesn't matter what you say, just that you maintain an upbeat tone. If your dog makes eye-contact with you, double down by saying "Treat!" or "Good Girl!" in a pleasant, deliberate, optimistic Daddy-voice, followed by giving her a treat.

Your Voice Says One Thing But the Leash Says Another
It won't work to be verbally positive but to be gripping the leash with white knuckles assuming the worst. Your whole presence needs to stay positive. The leash is kept loose and your pace doesn't change. If the dog seems oblivious to your speech or gets fixated on the other dog, you may want to put very slight tension on the leash just to say "Hey, remember me?" and continue your Daddy-speak. If your tone or energy turns, the dog's energy will probably turn as well. Your positive attitude can act as a counterbalance to their anxiousness.

Exercise: 11: Testing Your Dog's Reward Hierarchy

If you are going to reward, what are small rewards and what are large rewards? That depends on your dog. It would be helpful to know, so let's find out.

1. Assemble a collection of things to test: kibble, training treats, cheese, hot dog, peanut butter - whatever foods you might use to treat the dog - plus her favorite toys: rope toys, balls, chew toys, etc. You will need multiples for the food rewards but only one toy for each.
2. Fill the lower chart's first row and first column like the one below but with things you think *your* dog will really like:

Reward	Kibble	Treats	Hot dog	Cheese	Rope	Chew toy	Ball
Kibble	x						
Treats		x	Hot dog				
Hot dog		Hot dog	x				
Cheese				x			
Rope					x		
Chew toy						x	
Ball							x

Reward							
	x						
		x					
			x				
				x			
					x		
						x	
							x

3. Test each reward against all the others in the following manner:
   a. Ask the dog to sit
   b. Show her what you have in each hand and let her smell both items
   c. Step back, keeping her in a sit
   d. Hold your hands in front on your body and slightly out to the sides such that the rewards are about two feet apart from each other
   e. Release the dog ("Okay!")

      f. Note which reward she goes for.
      g. Repeat using the same two rewards but switching hands.
      h. If the dog goes for the same reward, once in your left hand, once in your right, write the name of that reward in the intersecting boxes on the chart (bacon is used as an example above). If the dog goes for the same hand twice, repeat the test until you can confidently determine which reward is preferred. In the example above, you can see I recorded "hot dog" as the winner over "treats".
      i. Continue until the chart is full.
      j. Look at your results. There should be a clear order of preferred rewards.

4. Notes:
      a. This should be fun for you and really fun for the dog.
      b. It might be helpful to have another person record the data while you administer the test to the dog

Takeaway

If we can interrupt the connection between a situation and the negative feeling our dog has about it, we can reprogram or counter-condition our dog to feel (and behave) in a different manner: our response, demeanor and behavior can challenge old patterns. Also, understanding reward hierarchy is helpful in matching the right reward with the situation: low value rewards are for everyday/easy situations and high value rewards are reserved for more stressful or more important situations.

Chapter 12: Disagreements

When people speak to other people, in most situations they use a common verbal language to express all kinds of ideas and concepts. When dogs speak to other dogs, much of the communication is physical rather than verbal. When people interact with dogs, the body language we often pair with a verbal command (such as raising an open upturned palm as we say "sit") is often the more effective part of our inter-species communication. Watch dogs play for a while and you will see more communication than you hear.

Canine communication is binary: yes or no, agree or disagree. "Bella, sit." If she sits, "Good girl," and the conversation ends. If she does not sit, we can disagree: with a move towards her, a slight increase in volume or with a more deliberate tone."Uh-uh... Bella. Sit." A similar conversation without speech might look like this:

1. Person looks at dog and raises open upturned palm to indicate sit.
2. If dog sits, person gives treat or affection, then walks away.
3. If dog does not sit, person disagrees by stepping closer to the dog. Dog may then back into a sit.

Disagreement:
Keep the conversation going (follow through) until the dog gives the desired behavior
- ❏ Move towards the dog
- ❏ Lean forward
- ❏ Physically block the dog's path with your body
- ❏ Get louder or more deliberate (not angrier)

Agreement:
End the conversation
- ❏ Move away from the dog
- ❏ Give praise or reward
- ❏ When you don't disagree you may be passively agreeing, implying that it is acceptable for the bad behavior to continue

Follow-Through to a Change in Intensity
Imagine the following scenario. The doorbell rings and the dog launches into hyperactivity: Over Threshold, super excited, barking and jumping at the closed front door. Without speech, you position yourself between the dog and the door. Facing the dog, you slowly move forward, removing access to the door by backing the dog up with your body. The dog backs into a sit but is still very excited.

If you were to step away from the dog, she would probably get up and go right back to mania. The expert move here and in many situations is *following through to a change in intensity*. What does that mean? Remain standing in front of the dog. This conversation is still in process. Wait for the shift: the dog's tail stops wagging or the dog lays down or the dog shifts itself into a more relaxed sit (often her bottom shifts laterally). If you then take a step back and she stays calm, you are agreeing with her change in behavior. If she jumps right back up, re-enter the conversation and disagree again.

When you then open the door to greet your guest, there may be another round of disagreement if the dog gets up. Sometimes, a single step towards the dog is enough to remind her of what you are looking for. At other times, it may involve backing her up further until she shows you the drop in intensity again.

As mentioned before, a dog can be "excited obedient" which is like tapping the pause button, whereas "calm obedient" is more like pressing stop. If the dog's intensity level drops, the likelihood of continued disobedience drops as well.

Avoidance
Sometimes, the dog will go into avoidance, trying to exit the conversation without giving the desired behavior. Avoidance may take a number of different forms:
- ❏ Leaving the room or area
- ❏ Picking up a toy or other distraction
- ❏ Trying to interact with another person (if one is in the vicinity)
- ❏ Trying to interact with another dog (if one is in the vicinity)

This may be fine for you. The dog is no longer focused on the door. Or, you may want to continue your follow-through until you see her intensity drop, by disagreeing with this new avoidant behavior. Often the process will look like this:
1. Doorbell rings
2. Hyperactive dog, jumping and barking (Over Threshold)
3. Person disagrees
4. Avoidant dog, picks up toy, paces around (Engaged)
5. Person disagrees
6. Obedient dog, sits or lies down (Balance)
7. Person agrees

Marking Disagreements
The clicker provides a distinct sound to announce that a reward is imminent. This is used in classical conditioning, like Pavlov's bell. Similarly, it is possible to pair a sound with an imminent disagreement or behavioral request. My marker of choice is snapping my fingers once. I am saying to the dog, "Hey. I want your attention. I am in disagreement with your current behavior so look at me and I will show you what I want from you."

Blocking
Blocking is simply getting in between the dog and whatever it is you don't want her to get to (guest, stranger, the cat, another dog, a piece of food that fell on the floor, etc.). It is a form of physical communication but is in no way violent.

Herding
Herding is something dogs do to sheep, small children, other dogs and puppies. Think of it as a directive form of blocking. "I don't want you over here. I want you over there. If you try to go around me, I will move to block you again. I'm going to leave the desired path open to you. When you go that way, I will stop herding you." For example, if the dog is a little too energetic to be in the house, herd her to the back door so she can run around in the back yard. Often I will also point in the direction I want her to go to reinforce my intention.

Claiming Space
Related to blocking and herding is claiming space. You can claim a few feet in front of the door where you don't want the dog to be or you can claim the entire room except for the dog bed in the corner. The process is the same as above: block and herd until the dog is out of the claimed space. When she moves

away from the door or goes to her dog bed, the disagreement is over. Dogs understand territory in terms of energy. "When I go over there, Daddy disagrees, but when I stay here or go the other way, we're good." Claim the same space repeatedly over time and you will see the dog will quickly understand, "Okay, I'm supposed to stay away from the door again."

Claiming Other Resources
Similar to space, you can claim toys, food or access to an activity. Same concept. This object belongs to you the person, until you choose to give it to the dog. Place a desired object (toy, treat etc) on the floor a few feet away from the dog. When the dog moves toward the object, block her. She may try to go around. Continue to deny the dog access to the object. When she gives up and stops trying to get to it, then you can give her access to the object. She gets it when she stops trying to get it. Got it?

"This one goes to eleven." *(a reference to the movie, "This Is Spinal Tap")*
Having the ability to modulate your intensity up or down to fit the situation is not only helpful, it may be necessary. If it is late at night and your dog is tired and not responding to your request to go outside before bed, her energy level might be a two on a scale from one to ten. To disagree with her, you only need to be a three. On the other hand, if your dog is riled up and mouthy, she might be a seven which would require you being an eight. On rare occasions, you might need to go to eleven to disagree with her when she's at a ten. It would be cruel to go to eleven when she's at a two and ineffective to be at a two when she's at a ten; use *just enough energy to disagree successfully*.

Exercise 12: Disagreements

Blocking / Claiming Space:

1. Draw an imaginary line four feet away from the front door (or if you would prefer, create an actual line with a piece of tape). Have someone ring the bell or knock from outside.

2. Assuming the dog runs to the door, step in front of her and use your body to move the dog to the other side of the line.

3. The dog is allowed to do anything so long as she stays behind the line, but she only receives a treat when she has calmed down. Wait through any avoidance behaviors for the change to calm. It may take seconds or minutes.

4. Open the door. If the dog stays calm, treat her. If she gets up, wait until she is back to calm before treating her. If you need to block or claim space again, do so.

5. Repeat on a regular basis until the dog knows what is expected of her when the doorbell rings.

Herding (similar to above but going a step further)

6. Draw an imaginary line four feet away from the front door. Have someone ring the bell or knock from outside.

7. Assuming the dog runs to the door, step in front of her and use your body to move the dog to the other side of the line.

8. Continue to walk the dog back with your body to a dog bed on the other side of the room. Interrupt any avoidant behavior and keep the disagreement going until the dog sits or lays down on the bed and is calm.

9. Open the door. If the dog stays calm and in her bed, treat her. If she gets up, herd her to the bed again and then treat her.

10. Repeat on a regular basis until the dog knows what is expected of her when the doorbell rings.

Takeaway
Disagreements are a way to discourage a behavior without "punishing" the dog. It is possible to disagree with the behavior and then agree with the follow through to a calm state. Also, disagreements can be marked (with a finger snap or "uh-uh!") similar to how we mark rewards (with a clicker).

Chapter 13: The Importance of Timing

While people (most of the time) have the ability for reason and perspective, dogs live in a world still very much connected to their Situation-Feeling-Behavior pictures and their fight or flight response. The advantage to the dog's system is speed; the disadvantage: little to no real cognition. Without being slowed down by higher reasoning, your dog may act instinctively instead of waiting for you to figure things out.

Human's reaction:
"Hmm. Bella sees that man walking towards us, and while I don't see him doing anything to indicate aggression, I know she sometimes has issues with people wearing hats (come to think of it, just men), so maybe I should do something to let her know she is safe..."

Dog's reaction: *10 times faster*
"There's a man in a black hat. He's too close!!! Bark bark bark!"

Bella is reacting well before her owner has finished processing what is happening.

When We Do What We Do Is As Important As What We Do
In many situations we have *less than a second* to interrupt our dog's automatic behavior. Can we do it? Sure we can. We just need to be alert and to know what to look for. Ears perk up and body goes rigid? What are you going to do? Dog crouches and tail goes down? The clock is ticking. If you're texting or checking your email, it probably already happened (...what happened? Exactly).

Very soon after an event has ended, the connection to what came before becomes tenuous at best. Reward after the fact is useless and confusing. It may feel good to you to treat your dog but the dog doesn't learn anything. Punishment after the moment has past is useless, as well as mean.

Click/Treat
Click and reward also needs to be swift. If you don't have your clicker at the ready, don't click. If you have the clicker at the ready but will then fumble around finding the treat, don't click. Click and immediately deliver the reward. If you would prefer to use a vocal cue and then treat, the same timing rules apply: Say "Treat!" right at the moment when you want to reinforce her behavior or mental state, then give her the treat right away. You may wait between a command and the click if you are working on duration, but once the click comes, the treat follows immediately.

For example: "Lulu, sit.... wait... ... ..." <click> and deliver treat.

Dogs Meeting Dogs
When your dog meets a new dog, the time it takes for the two to determine what kind of encounter it will be is also very short. When you see a scene like the one pictured in the following graphic, the dogs may be deciding what to do next. Two well socialized dogs off-leash will probably sort things out fine by themselves, but leashed dogs may not behave as well. The leash removes the option for a dog to create distance. Without that option, a dog may be more fearful, the energy level of the situation may increase and there could be a show of aggression or fear, or both. If your dog is meeting another dog that neither of you know, limit this moment to just a second or two and then start moving again. That may seem too quick for you, but you are a person and your dog is a dog; what is good for the goose is not always good

for the gander. Not all dogs like all other dogs. If either dog is uncomfortable, best to keep things moving.

Graphic 13.1

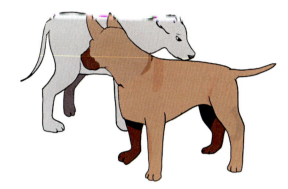

Exercise 13: Timing

1. Bring a friend along when you walk your dog in an area with distractions. Ask your friend to look ahead and keep an eye on what's going on and to keep you safe. For example, your friend might let you know that a car was approaching or that there were a group of kids coming up to the right of the path.

2. Focus on your dog and try to read her reactions. Can you catch the moments when her body language changes? Is she excited, scared, or vigilant? How can you tell? What changes can you see? (Refer to Chapter 3: Body Language if you need a reminder.)

3. What do you think is up ahead? Can you guess without looking? Something your dog likes or something your dog is concerned with?

4. For the second half of the walk, ask your friend to calmly announce anything the dog might find interesting as soon as your friend sees it. For example: "Big dog ahead," "Squirrel to the right," etc.

5. Watch your dog and see if you can sense the moment when she sees the object of interest as well. Extra credit if you can predict her body language before she shifts.

Takeaway

Our observation and reaction skills need to be sharp because dogs can think and react faster than we can. But if we are alert before our dog is alert, we have a chance of making up the difference in reaction time. With fearful or reactive dogs, honing our timing can be invaluable.

Chapter 14: Putting it All Together

Much of this workbook has led up to this chapter. We have looked at understanding what is happening, why it is happening, when it is happening, knowing how we need to be and knowing what we need to do. Below is a possible hierarchy of tactics to address an unwanted behavior. We will use the "man in a black hat" example from previous chapters.

What we are starting with:

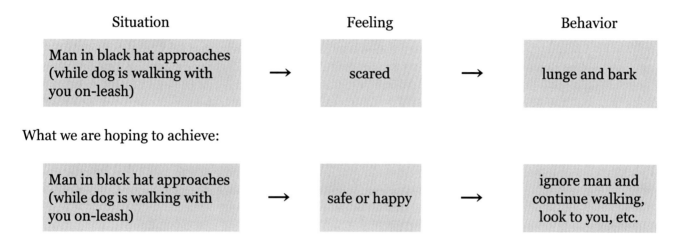

What we are hoping to achieve:

So when our dog sees a man in a black hat, her existing picture is connected to fear, which predicates lunging and barking. If we can reprogram the connection between the situation and the feeling, we may change the feeling and therefore the behavior. As mentioned in the previous chapter on timing, we may have less than a second to work with. We are not trying to change the behavior (lunging and barking) directly: *we are trying to prevent it.*

The Pre-Emotional Interrupt
We want to change the connection to the man in the black hat from scary to safe or happy. We want the dog to reassociate men in black hats with a new picture. This can be done with the tools from Chapter 11 (counter-conditioning and projecting positive emotion... "Clowns and Chocolate"). Use your own positive emotional state coupled with a high value reward to change the emotion of the situation *before* your dog references the old picture. "Oh look! A man in a black hat! Everything is going to be okay. What a good girl you are! Here's a treat!" You might hold the treat right in front of her nose as you walk by the man, or give her multiple treats in rapid succession. The goal is that she is still aware of the man but through your intervention the association with him becomes less scary and more enjoyable.
Parenting style: it might look and sound like Mommy but it's actually more Mom

The Pre-Behavioral Interrupt
Dogs display their emotional state almost transparently through body language. If the dog still shifts body language despite your attempt to interrupt as described above, it is time to interrupt before the unwanted behavior (lunging and barking) starts. You see the dog's body language change, and *in that instant* it's Carrot *and* Stick from Chapter 10. Correct by snapping your fingers or saying "Uh-uh!" Request a new behavior - "Let's go this way!" and Reward by giving praise or a treat. Again, timing is of the utmost importance. Essentially what you are telling your dog is, "I disagree with how you are feeling about that man and I know what you are likely to do, so how about instead you do this and I will reward

you for it?" Doing this consistently still has the power to change the picture. When the dog sees the man in the black hat, she will start expecting you to ask for an alternate behavior which results in a reward.
Parenting Style: Mom

The Mid-Behavioral Interrupt

If the above two strategies do not alter the unwanted behavior, the third line of defense is to interrupt the lunging and barking *at the exact moment* when she decides to "do something." Your dog probably has a "tell": something subtle she does right before she lunges. Is is a fixed stare? The hair on her back raises? Does she slow down? Our goal is to break focus. Imagine if you were winding up to throw a baseball and just as you were releasing the ball, I reached over and squeezed your nose, or I yelled something unexpected like, "RHINOCEROS!" I'll bet you would have a hard time throwing the ball effectively, if you were able to release it at all.

So what can you do to interrupt the behavior as it is about to happen? I often find that my intensity (not anger) can break the moment. Often, this just means being louder and more deliberate in my own behavior. What I am talking about is difference between "Tickle, treat!" and "TICKLLLLLE, TREAT!" or "Tickle let's go this way," and "LET'S GO!" I will often also change our trajectory by walking at a slight angle away from the man in the hat instead of directly towards him. My goal is for my communication to break through Tickle's focus. The *moment* she becomes disinterested in the man in the black hat, I reward her. I want her to learn that I disagree with her *intention* to act. The more I prevent the behavior, the less likely it will repeat.
Parenting style: Between Mom and Mother

The interrupts above are designed to *change the connection* between Situation, Feeling and Behavior. There may be times, for whatever reason, that implementation might be difficult or impossible: you're tired, the man in the black hat catches you off guard, you don't have treats with you, etc.. In those situations, having strategies to *interrupt the situation* will be quite useful.

The Management Interrupt

In management, we're downgrading from "teachable moment" to "let's just get through this safely." Another way of saying this would be that we *change the situation* so that the feeling and behavior don't follow. Here are a number of ways to do this.

When you see the man in the black hat approaching:
1. Turn and walk in the other direction
2. Turn the dog 180° and ask her to sit
3. Drop treats off to the side of the path so she can sniff around for them
4. Walk around a visual barrier (like a car) when the man gets close
5. Say, "Excuse me sir. Sorry to bother you but my dog is afraid of black hats. Would you mind removing yours until we pass? Thank you so much."
6. Run instead of walk past the man in the black hat, decreasing the duration of the event

Parenting style: Mother (take control of the situation to maintain safety)

The Professional Interrupt

If after repeated attempts none of the above tactics produce the desired result, it may be time to bring in a professional to assist you: someone with experience working with dogs and reading their body language who can also look at your attempts and help you troubleshoot. Interspecies communication takes practice. Asking for help is okay. We are not perfect, and that's okay. Our dog's behavior probably isn't perfect either, and that's okay, too. You care enough to try. Keep at it. The rewards will come.

Exercise 14: Putting it All Together

1. The instructions are simple: implement the above hierarchy of interrupts and figure out what works with your dog. Record your results in the table below.

   If you aren't having much luck, increase the distance from whatever triggers her or reduce the duration of the event, then start again. Also, make sure she is calm before you begin. The more energy she starts with, the easier it will be for her to go Over Threshold.

Unwanted Behavior	What I Tried	Result

Takeaway

If possible, we want to interrupt the dog before the unwanted behavior appears. If we can change the dog's feeling about the situation, interrupt the connection between feeling and behavior, or change the situation such that it doesn't have a chance to trigger the feeling, the unwanted behavior will decrease in frequency or disappear.

Chapter 15: Choose Your Battles

Every human/canine relationship is unique. It is a healthy strategy to set goals that are realistic for both you and your dog. Some things may not be achievable. Some things may not *yet* be achievable due to your lack of experience or skill, and some other things may not *yet* be achievable due to the level of trust your dog has in your skill.

When in Doubt, Avoid
If you aren't ready to tackle a behavioral issue, don't. Bringing an aggressive dog to the dog park and hoping she'll come when called is a recipe for disaster. If you don't have a strategy and something bad could happen, do what you can to not get into that situation.

Manage
For any number of reasons, sometimes, managing a behavioral issue is as far as you and your dog will get. If you haven't yet found a successful strategy to change the behavioral issue, management is an appropriate choice. Management is not hiding from a situation but instead controlling the parameters such that under no circumstances does the dog go Over Threshold. This may mean increasing distance from triggers (the man in the black hat, other dogs, etc.), reducing duration of encounters and especially asking for what you need from other people and dog owners, etc.. "Is your dog friendly?" people may ask. Being able to say, "She's not so good with other dogs," or "She's scared of strangers." can be a wonderful tool to keep everyday situations from becoming uncomfortable, dangerous, or traumatic for your dog.

Medication would be another version of management. An anxious dog might benefit from taking a prescription. If medicating your dog is something you feel comfortable with, there may be value in managing her anxiety in that manner. Down the road you may find a permanent solution, but in the meantime, it is possible a pill could help. It is up to you and your vet.

Behavioral Repair/Modification/Reprogramming/Counter-Conditioning/Etc.
The processes of creating permanent changes in behavior will probably take the most work but yield the greatest results. A Consistent, Compassionate, Deliberate strategy to address a behavioral issue may take patience and skill. If you are up to the challenge, I applaud you (as does your dog).

You might ask why this chapter is near the end of the book and not the beginning. Well, in order to decide if you feel ready to address any of the challenges you are experiencing, it might be helpful to understand what some of the strategies might be. Now that you are (hopefully) more informed, let's take a look at the final exercise in the workbook: Choose Your Battles.

Exercise 15: Choose Your Battles

1. What situations or behaviors do you feel you would like to avoid addressing for the time being?

    _____
    _____
    _____

2. How do you plan to avoid these situations or behaviors?

    _____
    _____
    _____

3. What situations or behaviors would you prefer to manage for the time being?

    _____
    _____
    _____

4. How do you plan to manage these situations or behaviors?

    _____
    _____
    _____

5. What behaviors do you feel ready to really focus on and address?

    _____
    _____
    _____

Takeaway
We do not need to "fix" every problem today, or ever. Choose what you are willing to work on and avoid or manage the rest until you decide you are ready.

Bonus Chapter 16: Dog Geometry

There are a few things from the world of geometry that are helpful to know in regards to dogs. You don't need to know the Pythagorean Theorem; just keep a few simple concepts in mind.

Approach Vectoring
Many dogs don't like meeting other dogs head on. It can be confrontational. The worst approach for a dog is a long, straight approach on a narrow path. Do what you can to arc your trajectory so that there is always at least a small angle to the dogs' approach. If you can curve even a little from one side of the path to the other, do so. If your dog is very reactive, you might want to find wider paths for your walks.

Graphic 16.1

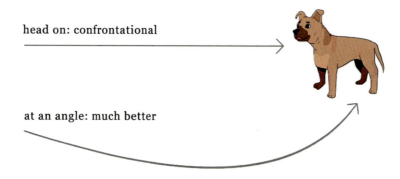

Parallel Walking
The safest way to introduce two dogs is to walk them next to each other and very gradually decrease the distance between them. You may need a large open space like a parking lot so that you can begin with the dogs at a distance where neither dog is barking or pulling. Start with dogs on the outside, people on the inside. If both dogs seem comfortable, slowly move closer together. If dogs still seem comfortable, switch the dogs to the inside, people on the outside while still maintaining safe distance at which the dogs cannot reach each other. If you see no signs of distress or reactivity, you might try letting one dog quickly sniff the other from behind, then swap, all while moving forward. Don't rush it. A long, slow, uneventful introduction beats a quick, reactive introduction any day.

Humans Approaching an Unknown Dog
Just like with dogs approaching other dogs, a head-on, dog-to-human approach is the most confrontational. Kneeling down, at a 90-degree angle (addressing the dog from the side), shows respect. Another uncomfortable approach is reaching over the dog's eyes to pet its head. Height equates to dominance, as does moving towards the dog. Your dog may not mind when you do these things because she knows you, but a strange dog may be agitated when a stranger does these things, or your dog may be agitated when a stranger greets her this way.

Three Units of Distance
For dogs, there is "here" (in *my* space, by invitation or by invasion), "just over there" (I'm quite alert to your presence and waiting to see what will happen next), and "way over there" (I see you but I don't really care who you are or what you are up to). At what distance do the transitions occur? That depends on your dog, and they can change over time. For Momo, "just over there" used to be anything more than a few feet up to about thirty yards. Over time, thirty yards reduced to about twelve feet. Can you figure

out where the transitions are for your dog? Look at her body language and intensity level as people or other dogs move closer and farther away.

Graphic 16.2

Leash Angle

If you need to change direction while walking your dog on-leash, try to do so by pulling sideways instead of from behind. Pulling from behind encourages the dog to pull forward. From the side or above is less confrontational. You may need to reset how you walk with the dog, specifically where the dog's body is in relation to your body or the carriage of your arm.

Leash Length

When walking on the street or in areas where you will meet people and other dogs, leash length is an important consideration. The longer the leash, the more momentum the dog can generate if it suddenly becomes interested in something. As a rule of thumb, A leash that allows the dog to roam within three to five feet of you is usually a good choice. That does not mean you just buy a five foot leash and call it a day. If you have a small dog, a five foot leash may be fine but with a larger dog, the connection point is higher. Also, your arm probably doesn't stay in a fixed position, so how you hold the leash will need to be considered. As an example, I often use a four foot leash with my dogs that are about two feet tall. It works well unless I use a front-connecting harness (which moves the connection point lower) and then the leash feels too short.

Graphic 16.3

Bonus Chapter 17: Miscellaneous Tips & Tricks

There are a few things I wanted to include that didn't seem to fit into the other chapters, so in conclusion I will list them here in no particular order.

Novel vs. Familiar
Dogs love rituals: seeing you go to the cabinet to get the dog food, going out to pee right before going to bed, etc. Sometimes, when some aspect of the situation is unfamiliar, the dog behaves unpredictably. If you teach the dog to sit in the backyard but never teach it to sit on a walk, the dog may not be as quick to comply as when you are at home. Here are a few things that could affect the consistency and predictability of a situation (and the emotion and therefore the behavior):
- Location (inside vs backyard vs dog park)
- Participants (new people, new dogs)
- Equipment (leash, harness)
- Health (itchy, injured, hungry, tired)
- Environment (weather, temperature, lighting)
- Distance (trigger/stimulus at twenty feet vs. five feet)
- Duration (pause vs. stay near this new/scary/unpleasant thing)

So, reteach the same skill (sitting, walking on a loose leash, etc.) in novel situations.

Fear of Missing Out (FOMO)
Many dogs worry when they are not included in an activity, or if their owner moves to another room or area without letting them know. "What might I be missing?" For some dogs, "follow" is more powerful than "come". Can you walk away from the dog when you want to go back in the house instead of walking towards her and trying to leash her? She may "fear" what she is missing out on if she believes you are leaving without her.

How We Leave the House Sets the Tone for the Walk
An interesting strategy is to wait for calm and obedient before going for a walk. Bring the dog to the door, leash her and ask her to sit. Open the door. Disagree with her if she tries to go out. When she is sitting with the door open, then you go out together to walk. Before you go out, she has to agree that she can't without your permission.

Walking With Purpose
When we give dogs a job, they often relax into obedience. If the dog's job is to "travel from here to there" with purpose, that may be enough to qualify as employment. I'm a big fan of setting a comfortable pace and sticking to it instead of slowing down and speeding up at the whim of the dog. If you want to stop to let the dog mark or sniff, feel free to do so, but when you start moving again, resume the previous pace. Stopped or walking: two discrete states. How much stopping to sniff? Depends if you're style is Mommy, Mom or Mother.

K9 Bridle™
Many people wonder what equipment they might use to walk a dog that pulls: a harness, flat collar, prong collar, etc.?" I've tried almost everything out there and one of my preferred tools is called the K9 Bridle. It is a head collar, similar to a Gentle Leader™, inspired by a bitless horse bridle but with two distinct differences. First, the connection to the leash is on the back of the head instead of under the chin. Second, there is a Martingale™ loop on the back of the head that gently tightens when the dog pulls. In comparison to a Martingale™ collar, choke collar or prong collar, the tightening happens on

the snout, head and chin instead of the dog's neck. For me, it gives a high level of control but without choking or prongs. The K9 Bridle™ is durable, easy to fit and easy to get used to. Similar to the Gentle Leader™, some people at first think it looks like a muzzle but I tell them, "It's really more of a steering wheel for my strong energetic dogs." The K9 Bridle™ is made in the UK and can be ordered online at http://www.k9bridle.com.

Attention, Then Communication
Using the dog's name or saying, "Hey, you" is not a request for behavior. We may need to first get the dog's attention, then we can communicate. If you can differentiate by tone what kind of communication it is, the dog will probably respond more consistently. It is possible to say "sit" deliberately ("Sit!"); it's also possible to say it almost as if it's a question ("Sit?"). *Tone trumps content with dogs.*
- ❑ To get attention: use the dog's name, whistle, clap, some other sharp, deliberate sound
- ❑ To request: deliberate, confident tone ("Sit!")
- ❑ To correct: snap fingers and/or use a mildly abrasive sound ("Uh-uh!")
- ❑ To give affection: warm, positive and deliberate ("Good girrrl!")

"Touch": My Favorite Command
The "touch" command (sometimes called "target") is my favorite dog command for a number of reasons. It is easy to teach, can be used long-distance, relies more on body language than speech, and it can replace "come", "follow" and even "drop it" in some situations.

Stand with your arms straight down by your sides, then with a flat open palm facing forward, raise that arm out to the side to form a 45 degree angle with your body. Your hand will be about 15 inches away from your thigh. When the dog touches your hand with her nose, she receives a treat. "Touch" can be taught very quickly with a clicker. I'm actually a fan of holding the treat in that hand, which adds an element of scent luring.

Anytime the dog sees your body shape (standing with your arm out to the side) it means "treat". She has to go to you to get the treat ("come"), follow you if you are moving away ("follow") or drop a toy to eat the treat ("drop it" or "let go"). And, in low light your silhouette still works because dogs see in shapes and this shape is very easy to pick out.

The Muzzle Correction
Dogs asserting dominance, including mothers with their puppies, may wrap their mouth around the muzzle of another dog. This is not intended to inflict damage; it serves to confirm the social statuses in the relationship or as a correction. The human equivalent would be to hold your hand in the form of a claw and press your hand against the dog's chin and side of its muzzle. I want to be absolutely clear: *this is not about hurting, jabbing or provoking the dog.* Just press with enough pressure to hold the dog's attention. (Note: Cesar Millan uses this technique on his tv show but with (in my humble opinion) way too much force and intensity. This is meant to be a disagreement, not an assault.)

An example where this technique might be appropriate is with a dog who is moving forward and doing something that is absolutely unacceptable, such as chasing the cat or getting mouthy with a child. An example where this technique is probably not appropriate is with a dog moving back and exhibiting fear or nervousness, as you may feel invasive to a dog who is already seeking distance. We'll use chasing the cat as an example.

Create a scenario where the dog can see the cat but not get to the cat. (You might use a gate or other barrier with one person holding the cat and the other working with the dog.) Leash or tether the dog, just in case. Assuming the dog fixates on the cat, stand between the dog and cat. If the dog motions to go or look around you, claw her muzzle and hold pressure until she stops looking at the cat. This might be a few seconds or a few minutes. *The dog may appear confused or unsure; this is a good sign. It means the dog is learning something new* (to break with instinct and stop chasing the cat). Follow through. This disagreement lasts until the dog turns her gaze away from the cat, at which moment you can calmly say "Good girl" ("Not that, this" from Chapter 10). Repeat on a regular basis until the dog no longer shows interest in the cat. The dog thinking of the cat as a toy is not allowed. We want the dog to get that message loud and clear. The short term discomfort can help create a lasting, long term comfortable state (in which no cats are eaten).

As with any time you are putting your hand near a dog's mouth, use caution and common sense. If you think there is even a remote chance of your dog biting you, this method may not be appropriate.

I debated for quite a while whether to include the muzzle correction in this workbook. People who don't understand it see it as violent. I do not believe that it is. It is a stern disagreement. To put it in context, my dogs sometimes "mouth wrestle" with each other, as many dogs do. Their faces are in each others' mouths during play. It doesn't mean they hate each other. There is no wounding or blood (though sometimes Momo's head is soaking wet from Tickle's saliva). The muzzle correction is less dangerous and less physical than how they treat each other. I would also say it is less emotionally violent than yelling at a dog. Remember, it is an option, not a required practice, and if it doesn't feel right to you, don't use it.

Graphic 17.1

Pack Walks
If your dog needs work on being around other dogs, look in your area for *on-leash* pack walks. You may find them on meetup.com or through local dog trainers. These walks will offer the opportunity for controlled desensitization. Being around other dogs is the only way your dog will become comfortable being around other dogs. Maintain safe distance, expect there will be some barking and/or pulling and let the "power of the pack" and the purposeful migratory pace do its magic. The primary purpose is not for your dog to meet other dogs but to be in close proximity to other dogs. If at the end of the walk your dog and another dog are calm, this may be the time for a quick controlled greeting.

Effective "Recall"
In Ken Ramirez's Advanced Dog Training Topics seminar, he describes an effective recall as, "when cue sounds, animal should stop everything and come immediately back to trainer." The concept is simple, yet this remains elusive for many pet owners. The keys are:
- **Use a unique sound**. It needs to be easily recognizable from other noises. An electronic bird call or a whistle would be good if you're not in an area where these items are frequently used.

- **Create a call that is unique to you and your dog and deliver it consistently.** For example, Olive's recall is three quick blasts on the whistle then I loudly and cheerfully say her name: "<tweet tweet tweet> Olive!" For those of you who watch the TV show "The Big Bang Theory", Olive's recall is rhythmically similar to how Sheldon knocks three times on Penny's door and then says, "Penny?"
- **Continue making the sound until dog is moving rapidly back to you.** Don't sound it once and hope for the best.
- **The reward for returning needs to be very high.** If you normally use kibble for rewards, this needs to be much more desirable: cooked chicken, dried liver, etc..
- **Never skimp on the reward.** The recall signal *always* results in a great treat.
- **Do not use recall to reprimand the dog or to end play/leave the dog park.** Recall must alway connect to a positive experience.
- **Practice in as many locations and as often as you can.** You might start in the house, then move to the back yard, then start on a walk through the forest with a long dragging leash as a safety backup. Once your dog is reliable, keep the frequency of use low in easy locations and high in more challenging locations: only do recall once in awhile in the house but use it multiple times when you go for a hike).

Your Secret Weapon: The Flirt Pole
A flirt pole is an excellent tool to help exercise your dog. It consists of a pole with a piece of rope attached to one end with a toy tied to the other end of the rope. Essentially, it's a fishing pole for dogs. You can purchase them online or make your own from parts at the hardware store. There is a video at www.canine-strategies.com if you'd like to see my homemade flirt pole in action.

Entice your dog to chase the toy at the end of the rope. You can walk or run or just stand in one place and rotate. Try to keep the toy just out of reach most of the time to keep her chasing it. When she does catch the toy, ask her to drop it and trade for a treat. (If she isn't dropping it, the treat may not be of high enough value.) Ask her to sit, then release her by saying "Okay!" at the same moment as you begin moving the flirt pole again.

Why is the flirt pole is a secret weapon? It allows you to train, exercise, mentally stimulate and modulate your dog's energy intensity, *all at the same time.*

Final Takeaway

- Emotion - Direction - Intensity - The Ring of Fire
- Body Language
- Preconditions
- Calm Obedient
- Mommy, Mom, and Mother - Deliberate, Compassionate, and Consistent
- Confidence
- Detective Work - Situation-Feeling-Behavior
- Reinforcement and Punishment - Carrot and Stick - The Power of Positivity - Disagreements
- Timing
- Putting It All Together
- Choosing Your Battles
- Dog Geometry - Miscellaneous Tips

We've covered quite a bit. Try something. If it works, do more of it. If it doesn't, try something else. Be kind, be safe, good luck, and have fun.